UNITY AND
JESUS FORSAKEN

Chiara Lubich

UNITY AND
JESUS FORSAKEN

New City Press

Published in the United States by New City Press
the Publishing House of the Focolare
206 Skillman Avenue, Brooklyn, NY 11211
©1985 by New City Press, New York

Translated from the original Italian edition
L' Unità e Gesú Abbandonato
©1984 Città Nuova Editrice, Rome, Italy
by Julian Stead, *o.s.b.*
Introduction translated by M. Angeline Bouchard.

Library of Congress Catalog Number: 85-072397
ISBN 0-911782-53-2
Printed in the United States of America

CONTENTS

INTRODUCTION

The pages of this book are filled with light. They were written by God through the wisdom of the Spirit within the soul of a woman who has revealed with purity and a sense of ecclesial responsibility the treasures she has received. And so they are given to the Church as a lofty and urgent message in which are joined two indissoluble realities that call to mind two decisive moments in the life of Jesus: his priestly prayer for unity (Jn 17:21-23); his cry of abandonment on the cross (Mt 27:46).

In the unlabored simplicity of true and essential realities, we speak of them in these terms: Unity and Jesus Crucified, Forsaken.

In a letter written in 1948, Chiara Lubich expressed with simplicity her experience of being inspired by the Lord about these two inseparable elements of Christian spirituality: "The book of light that the Lord is writing within my soul has two aspects—a page shining with mysterious love: Unity. A page luminous with mysterious suffering: Jesus Forsaken. They are two sides of a single coin."

The Focolare has been living by these two pages of light for more than forty years now, for it has been *rooted in love for Jesus Forsaken and been working for unity within and outside of the Church. The evangelical radicalism of the love that distinguishes it, Pope John Paul II has recently said, is constantly being vivified by these two keystones of its spirituality.**

In this book as nowhere else Chiara has revealed to us God's mysterious plan with respect to Unity and Jesus Forsaken. It is a reconstruction of experiences, a collection of simple texts—letters and notes—which as a splendid mosaic give form to these two realities, which were originally written with the fire of the Spirit so many years ago in Chiara's heart and in the hearts of her companions, the initial group of this movement of unity. They have now become the legacy of the whole Church and of humanity.

Like the words of the Gospel, like the most beautiful and genuine things in the Church's experience, these pages are presented in the form of a kind of "narrative theology," a simple and genuine account of the discovery of a great Ideal that has fascinated thousands upon thousands of men and women in our time throughout the world. They are experiences of life; they are not ideas, beautiful as these may be, but a reality to be lived—a reality that is understood better through life within the Church and that is destined to fulfill Jesus' Testament: "that all may be one."

* Cf. L'Osservatore Romano, *August 20-21, 1984, p. 5; also* Città Nuova, *XXVIII (1984), No. 17, p. 37.*

Unity and Jesus Forsaken, in their inseparable reciprocity, constitute a genuine novelty in Christian spirituality. They are a revelation, a charism, a gift to the Church of our time that is so open to the mystery of unity and so eager to discover, in a world such as ours, the face and the heart of Jesus Forsaken present within humanity.

These very lofty words of the Gospel, Unity and Jesus Forsaken, are a revelation of the Word Incarnate, of Jesus the only Teacher, but also a revelation from the God who is Love within the unity of the Trinity, which he wants to communicate to the world through the unfathomable depths of identification with humanity revealed in the cry of the Forsaken One. As pinnacles of Jesus' experience, they are not simply aspects of Christian spirituality to be considered along with others, but the very apexes of the Gospel in which all the originality of Christ's message shines forth.

As apexes and syntheses of Christian spirituality, Unity and Jesus Forsaken embrace all the broad outlines of evangelical spirituality, illuminate them, and have the power to reinsert them into the harmony of God's plan. They are universal principles that can be lived by everyone, in all vocations, and make it possible to live directly on a personal and communitarian level along the wavelength of the Spirit of Jesus. That is to say, to share his own sentiments of love, in the indissoluble experience of death and resurrection, in the continuous and luminous transition from suffering to love, in union with the very Spirit of the Crucified-Risen One.

Chiara's book begins by speaking of unity and concludes likewise with a chapter, which I would call prophetic, on unity. These are pages shining with the mysterious love of God, throwing light on the Lord's plan for our world, hungry and eager for unity at all levels, even amid the contradictions of manifold divisions. However the central chapters of the book speak of Jesus Forsaken who is precisely the key to unity, the model, the apex, the author of unity between God and mankind, between heaven and earth, between individual men and women and nations.

In this magnificent interweaving that corresponds to the very plan of salvation, unity is rediscovered as the divine life to be lived now within the Church, according to the desire and prayer of Jesus: "May they all be one. Father, may they be one in us, as you are in me and I am in you" (Jn 17:21).

Thus is rediscovered Jesus' "consecration" to the Father even to the abandonment of the Cross, as an absolutely necessary passage to attain the unity that Christ himself has given us together with his Spirit, poured out upon the Church, from his heart pierced by the most intense pain, in the loftiest and most pure love that has ever throbbed in the heart of man.

Unity. *In the midst of war, in air raid shelters, Chiara, with her young friends who were already following her, reread the Gospel by the light of a candle. She was deeply moved by a page that manifested all the majestic and sculpturesque truth of God's Word: John's*

10

Chapter 17, the prayer of unity. She understood through a supernatural intuition that this is what they were born for, and it was this that they were called to live in the Church, for the "May they all be one," as it is summed up for us in an evangelical slogan that henceforth possessed their hearts. John's words, read and reread, lived and commented upon, illumined one another and became the key to the understanding of all the other words of the Gospel.

It was a wonderful discovery. In a flash she understood that the life of God, the Trinitarian life, is unity: "As you are in me and I am in you..." And that this must become the life of all Christians who can and must live the very "way" of the Trinity.

The experience of such a life that impels us to live for one another, with one another, "making ourselves one" with our neighbor, raises our life to a continual and wonderful supernatural level, to a height where love is the supreme law, the primary and indispensable condition of all other actions. By living in God, by living God's own life, we discover how God sees and wants things to be, through a connaturality that springs from this love within the unity that consists in living the way the Trinity lives.

There is no doubt that a supernatural wisdom, a charism of the Holy Spirit lay at the basis of such a new and lofty discovery, which, I might say, was practically unknown, unheard of up to that moment in the Church; even though it had been sensed and preached in Christian spirituality. It can be affirmed that here we are in the presence of a charism born from a page

11

of the Gospel which in this instance is not the page of poverty, of prayer, or of the works of mercy, but the page that reveals the mystery of unity, the very purpose of Christ's coming among men, of his death and Resurrection.

Unity, the life of God, the ultimate standard of life, has as its effect the desire and the obligation to be like Jesus, to be Jesus, to live like him and in him, to allow oneself to live through him in order to be able to live the divine life. It involves the fundamental decision to die so that Jesus may live. But it is also the deeply moving communitarian experience of a new relationship with "the other," with others, of Jesus with Jesus, in order that we may die together so that 'Jesus in our midst" may be the life of all.

A spiritual and theological logic is the dependable foundation of all the experiences and intuitions that Chiara has had and written down concerning unity, and they also have the savor of innovation, the wonder of newness. Yes, this is an innovation that raises communitarian and ecclesial spirituality to the level of a Trinitarian spirituality, a spirituality of the unity in which love, and hence the demands of love, are endowed with a Trinitarian dimension: "as you are in me and I am in you."

This charismatic experience has ushered in the hour of unity into the Church, a communitarian and ecclesial spirituality of "the Mystical Body." It was indeed the dawn of a new era for the Church when, according to

12

the felicitous statement of R. Guardini, this dawn was breaking within souls. It was precisely in that year, 1943, the year the Focolare was born, that Pope Pius XII published his Encyclical Letter on the Church: Mystici Corporis.

This spirituality of unity bore within it the seeds of an innovation in Christian life, in asceticism, in the apostolate, indeed, in mysticism itself. It made new demands that could no longer be measured solely by the individual demands of Christian perfection, but needed to be measured against the very goal of the spiritual life which would now be envisioned as the holiness of God, Father, Son, and Holy Spirit, and hence as a communitarian holiness of the Trinitarian stamp, and therefore an ecclesial holiness.

Chiara Lubich, in her record of this discovery, has revealed to us the novelties that God had been gradually writing in her heart and in those of her companions whom she drew together as "one" with these realities she was coming to understand, and which she lived and communicated to them. It was an innovation verified in the demands of a new life and in the fruits produced by this evangelical life, which, by letting Jesus live in each one and in all, produced the extraordinary supernatural gift of the presence of Jesus in their midst (cf. Mt 18:20), the presence of the Risen One present in the group that lived within the Church and for the Church.

Jesus Crucified and Forsaken. *Chiara needed to make an additional discovery in order for unity not to be a* *utopia: Jesus Crucified and Forsaken, the author and model of the unity between God and people, and of people and one another.*

The discovery, the interior revelation, we might say, of this mystery has been impressed upon our memory by a date and a simple episode of life that is related in the pages of this book.

The date was January 24, 1944. When she asked: What was the greatest suffering of Jesus? a rather new and unusual answer was given. It penetrated Chiara's heart with the force of a flash of supernatural light: the moment when Jesus suffered most is expressed in his cry from the Cross: "My God, my God, why have you forsaken me? (Mt 27:46; Mk 15:34). From that moment on Chiara was fascinated by that cry. She penetrated "the passion of the passion of Jesus," the very soul of the one who, by becoming sin for us, experienced separation from God and cried out his deepest spiritual sufferings in which henceforth would be contained and fused all the possible sufferings of humankind.

It was only by a special grace of the Spirit that the torment of Jesus' cry won the attention and the love of Chiara for the Crucified, thenceforth bringing a deeper insight into an aspect that, although glimpsed for centuries within the Church, had not until that moment been given such spiritual importance. And it was quite natural from then on to give Jesus a new name: the Forsaken One, in order to gather up in the most acute suffering of his Passion and synthesize the discovery of the greatness of the love and the immensity

14

of the pain by which we have been redeemed and reconciled with the Father and among ourselves.

Free from any exegetical and theological prejudice or concern, with the wisdom of the little ones, Chiara attained to a deep understanding of the mystery of the abandonment of Jesus on the Cross. She understood that the spiritual suffering of Jesus was at once his great, immense love for the Father and his love for men, that it was the utmost limit of his human experience, abysmal identification with sin and with the sins of humankind. It was therefore necessary to love Jesus in this way within herself and in others, to embrace through love abandonments, torments, separations, and yet discovering the face and heart of the Forsaken One in all who suffer, discovering in every pain the spiritual experience of abandonment that is inherent in every human suffering.

The One who said: "To those who love me, I shall manifest myself" (cf. Jn 14:21) has continued little by little to reveal himself in the concreteness and universality of every face bearing the mark of pain. He presents himself as the Spouse to be loved and embraced in the sufferings of the Church, in the wounds of humankind, in every possible situation, even perhaps in the sin and denial of God within large strata of modern society. Sufferings no longer cause alarm but become a motive and an invitation to love more intensely, to embrace with prayer and witness each of

15

*these faces of Jesus Forsaken in order to make the
presence of God felt with love, the God who rejects no
one, who wills the salvation of all.*

*It can be affirmed that this discovery of the face of
Jesus Forsaken was prepared in advance in order to be
given to the Church of our time. Today, at the exegetical
and theological level, in spiritual and pastoral areas, the
wisdom of the Cross and the mystery of Jesus Crucified
in his abandonment arouse great interest. Catholic,
Orthodox, and Protestant theologians are fascinated by
this mystery. The theme of the suffering experienced
by Christ to its ultimate consequences also arouses the
interest of non-Christians and of all who are concerned
with the paradox of the Cross of Jesus. Around the Cross
of Christ are gathered all believers summoned by a cry
of pain and love that embraces everybody, that touches
the experience of every man and woman.*

*In these last few years as never before the same
Magisterium of the Church through the voice of Pope
John Paul II has called to mind this unfathomable
mystery. A page from the Apostolic Letter* Salvifici
Doloris *(No. 18) has admirably expressed this experience
of Jesus: "When Christ says 'My God, my God, why
have you forsaken me?' his words are not only the
expression of the abandonment that made itself felt
many times in the Old Testament, especially in the
Psalms—and in particular in Psalm 22 (21), from which
the words cited are taken. It can be said that these words
on abandonment are born at the level of the inseparable
union of the Son with the Father, and are born because*

the Father 'has laid on him the iniquity of us all' (Is. 53:6) and in accordance with what St. Paul was to say: 'For our sake God made him to be sin who knew no sin, so that in him we might become the righteousness of God' (2 Co 5:21).

Together with this horrible burden proportionate to the 'interior' evil of turning away from God that is inherent in sin, Christ, through the divine depth of his filial union with the Father perceived in a way that is humanly inexpressible this suffering that consists in separation, rejection by the Father, rupture with God. But precisely through such suffering he accomplished the Redemption and was able to say as he was dying: 'It is consumated' ...."

It is also Pope John Paul II who points to the mystery of the Cross as the key to unity and the valid response to the questions of all men and women who can discover that the sufferings of all humanity have been already lived by the Man of Sorrows. Quoting Pope John Paul II: "It is necessary nevertheless that all the sufferers who believe in Christ converge, and in particular those who suffer because of their faith in him, crucified and risen, so that the offering of their sufferings may hasten the fulfillment of the prayer of the same Savior for the unity of all. It is there that men of good will also converge, because on the Cross hangs the 'Redeemer of all,' the Man of Sorrows who has taken upon himself the physical and moral sufferings of the people of all times, so that they may find in love the salvific sense of their suffering and the valid answer to all their questions" (Salvifici Doloris, No. 31).

17

Chiara's pages on the mystery of Jesus Crucified and Forsaken can guide all people of good will to a deeper understanding of these authoritative expressions of the Magisterium of the Church, thereby contributing to their becoming an expression and norm of daily life.

The wide experience of many years has led to an insight and actuation of all the riches that lie hidden in this mystery and that are gradually explained with great clarity and simplicity throughout the pages of this book, so as to provide a key to the understanding of some fundamental aspects of the Christian mystery.

For example, it is understood that Jesus in his forsakenness is the definitive Word of the Father and the apex of Revelation; that he is the synthesis of all virtues and the fullness of holiness in love, because in this supreme instant he lives with unfathomable fullness obedient love for the Father and infinite charity for people.

Thus it is also understood that the One who cries out his forsakenness is also the One who with infinite filial trust commits himself into the hands of the Father: "Father, into your hands I commit my spirit" (Lk 23:46). And this is how Jesus accomplished a wonderful passage, a splendid Pasch, from the depths of abandonment to the serene trust of being welcomed into the Father's bosom, from death to life, from earth to heaven. It is the Pasch of the Forsaken One, who surrenders himself into the hands of the Father in order to emerge as the Risen One. Thus every Christian who lives this experience within himself and in others accomplishes a passage, a pasch of love that makes the joy of the risen ones flourish in his heart and on his face, the joy of those who like Jesus vanquish suffering with love.

Another wonderful discovery to which Chiara devotes several pages of lofty Trinitarian theology is the relationship between Jesus Forsaken and the gift of the Holy Spirit to the Church. It was from the heart of Christ, pierced by the centurion's lance, but really pierced by the suffering of his soul, that the very Spirit of Christ was poured out upon the Church. Jesus breathed out his Spirit (cf. Jn 19:30). From his side flowed blood and water (cf. Jn 19:34). The blood is the symbol of the life Jesus gave for his friends; the water is the sign of the Holy Spirit, the Trinitarian Love which is now being poured out upon the Church from the heart of Christ, so that the same love throbs in the Church that reigns within the Trinity through this gift that unites the human and the divine and enkindles all in this one love that can make of "many" one Body in one Spirit.

In this way Jesus Forsaken reveals the mystery of the Resurrection from which the Holy Spirit flows and efficaciously accomplishes, together with the gift of the Trinitarian life poured out on earth upon the Church of Pentecost, the mystery of unity, destined to bring fulfillment in accordance with Jesus' prayer at the Last Supper when God will be "all in all" (cf. 1 Co 15:28).

Jesus Forsaken is the soul of the Church, a way of saying with Paul: "For I decided to know nothing among you except Jesus Christ, and him crucified" (1 Co 2:2); "For me to live is Christ, and to die is gain"

19

(Ph 1:21). It is the very apex of Jesus' experience to which all Christians are called, baptized in his death and quickened by his Spirit. It is also the experience, an unconscious one perhaps, of everyone who through the Spirit's mysterious groanings opens himself through suffering to the Father of all. It is the life that unites in a love that is Trinitarian in nature all those who want to fulfill Jesus' New Commandment, loving one another as he has loved them.

Living Jesus Forsaken within us and in others leads to the joy of Easter, to a new love that can no longer fail, to the Risen One who lives in us and among us. We offer our hearts freely and unencumbered to the action of the Spirit of Pentecost. And thus we enter into the very dynamism of the Trinitarian life and of the plan of love of the Father, the Son, and the Spirit for the whole of humankind.

It is precisely on the foundation of this universal plan of salvation on which the unity of all men and women in Christ lies, that Chiara ends the pages of her book. To live Jesus Forsaken in order to actualize, to realize Jesus' Testament, his priestly prayer, the purpose of his redemptive death. To love the face of Jesus Forsaken in the problems and difficulties of the Church at every level, in the concreteness with which each one of us can discover this face in his or her own life and in the lives of others. To extend this love to all other Christians in a dialogue of love that can take on the burden of problems and difficulties in order to establish them in the truth and the love of Christ; allowing ourselves to

20

be guided by the Spirit and the Church. To open our hearts to all the faithful of the great religions, to the secularized humanity of our time, to the great masses far away from God who, although they do not know it, are a Crucified One who cries out his "Why?" and need a Church which, impelled by a love stronger than death, offers to all the revelation of a God who is Love.

In difficulties whether great or small, in personal sorrows and in social sufferings, in the wounds of humankind and in the problems of the Church, there emerges the face of Jesus Forsaken and an irresistible strength to love him in order to restore unity, to heal wounds, and to solve problems.

To achieve all this Chiara does not hesitate to propose the radicalism of love as a synthesis: "Behold: to love. To love all men and women, so that they all know what love is and love one another as Jesus wishes, this is the fervent desire of our movement."

Unity and Jesus Forsaken. Here are two words of light for the Church of our time, for all the people of our era, as we approach the year 2000 when the cry of the Forsaken is more urgent and the yearning for unity is more obvious at all levels of life.

These are words of hope that record the cry of pain from which the radiant dawn of Easter sprang, and the prayer of Jesus which will be mysteriously heard by the Father: "That all may be one." They are words which, as a gift of God for the Church, obligate all of us, disciples of Christ, to carry out in our time the

21

wonderful plan of unity for which Christ, in a cry of love and pain, offered his life and his Spirit.

Jesuś Castellano Cervera, OCD
Teacher of Spiritual Theology at the
"Teresianum" of Rome
Adviser to the Sacred Congregation
for the Doctrine of Faith

UNITY

We are all aware that the modern world is strikingly full of many kinds of tensions: between east and west, north and south; tensions in the Middle East and Central America; wars, threats of fresh conflicts, the explosion of various phenomena of terrorism and other typically contemporary evils. Despite all these tensions, one of the signs of the times is a trend towards unity.

One example of this, in the Christian world, comes from the Holy Spirit, stimulating the various Churches and ecclesial communities in the direction of reunion, after centuries of indifference and conflict. The Popes have spoken about it: Paul VI's teachings were filled with the idea of unity. John Paul II is now a true personification of this idea, as he makes his world-wide jouneys, his arms outstrechted to all its peoples.

The Second Vatican Council spoke of it; its documents keep returning to this thought, expressed in the consequent establishing of new secretariates, for Christian Unity, and for dialogue with other religions and with all people of good will.

Another sign is the World Council of Churches.

This tension towards unity in the world finds expression even in ideologies that we are not able to share, but which are striving to find a solution on a global scale to the great problems of today. It also expresses itself in international corporations and organizations; unity is likewise promoted by modern means of communication, which bring the whole world to a single community or family.

Yes, this pressure towards unity certainly exists in the world, and forms the context in which we should look at the Focolare and its spirituality.

Actually, whenever we are asked for a definition of our spirituality, or what difference there is between the gift of God to our movement and the gifts with which He has decorated and enriched others, in the Church today or of bygone centuries, we have no hesitation in replying: unity.

Unity is our specific vocation. Unity is what characterizes the Focolare. Unity, and none of the other ideas or words which, in one way or another, can stand for splendid and divine ways of going to God, as for instance "poverty" for the Franciscan movement, "obedience" perhaps for the Jesuits, "the little way" for followers of St. Thérèse of Lisieux, "prayer" for the Carmelites of St. Teresa the Great, and so on.

The word that epitomizes our spirituality is unity. For us, unity includes every other supernatural reality, every other practice or commandment, every other religious attitude.

If unity is typical of our vocation, let's take a quick look back to the beginnings of our forty-year history, when it was first kindled like a flame, so that we can keep it alive in our hearts, or revive it in case it needs reviving. Let us recall certain episodes, and read over again whatever we have preserved on this subject. A quick glance will help us to remain faithful disciples of the priceless gift God gave us.

Best of all, let's re-live some familiar episodes we remember from our earliest years. The war is on. A few girls and I are in a dark place somewhere—maybe a basement. We are reading the Testament of Jesus by candlelight. We peruse the whole passage. Those difficult words seem to light up, one after another. We feel like we understand them. But what we notice most of all is an inner conviction that they are the Magna Carta of this new life of ours and of all that is going to come into existence around us.

Some time later, conscious of the difficulty, if not impossibility, of putting such a program into practice, we feel the urge to ask Jesus for the favor of teaching us the way to live unity. Kneeling around an altar, we offer our lives to Him, that—if He wishes to, and trusts us—He may use them to bring it to pass. It is—as far as we remember—the Feast of Christ the King. We are struck by these words in the liturgy of the day: "Ask of me and I will give you the nations for an inheritance and the ends of the earth for your possession."[1] We ask, with faith.

Later on, with joy and astonishment, we will connect these events and our aspiration for unity with the encyclical which Pius XII launched into the world precisely in 1943, the year our movement was born: the encyclical "Mystici Corporis", on the Mystical Body of Christ.

One thing is clear in our soul: unity is what God wants of us. We only live to be one with Him, one with each other, and one with everybody. This marvelous vocation ties us to Heaven and plunges us into universal brotherhood. What could be greater? As far as we are concerned, no ideal in life beats this.

Let's go back to our earliest days again. We made a plan that every morning I would give the group of my first companions a short meditation in a room called the "Sala Massaia." We met at 7 o'clock. Inside myself I feel the urge not to ensnarl the Holy Spirit in my own thoughts, for if He thinks it worthwhile, He can enlighten me. So I prepare myself with prayer, declaring the "nothing" of me and the "all" of God: "I am nothing, You are everything," I say over and over to Jesus, in front of the Blessed Sacrament. After this prayer, I draw up a few notes. And this was God's chief system for forming the girls who were my first companions in this new ideal.

There is one left, from the notes of those years, going back probably to 1946, with a single topic, the one which matters most to the nascent movement: unity.

The text is very concise—those notes generally are. In it (after some words about the need for us to be another Jesus) God's program for us appears explicitly: Above all else, the soul must fix its gaze on the one Father of so many children. Next, look at all creatures as children of the one Father. Let our thoughts and hearts' affection always go beyond the bounds imposed by (merely) human life, and let's develop the habit of constantly reaching out to the universal brotherhood in only one Father: God."

And it goes on:

"Jesus, our model, taught us just two things, which are one: to be children of only one Father and to be brothers and sisters to each other."

One virtue is emphasized farther on, which is seen to be essential to union with God and with neighbor and which is mentioned by St. Paul in his letters, when he urges Christians to mutual love for the building of unity.

"A virtue"—the note continues—"which unites the soul with God . . . is humility, annihilation. The slightest human flaw which does not let itself be taken away by what is divine, breaks the union, and with grave consequences. The interior union of the soul with God presupposes the total extinction of self, humility to the most heroic degree. . . .

"Humility is also the way to arrive at 'primacy' by putting oneself at one's neighbor's service, so far as possible."

"Every soul which wants to achieve unity must claim only one right: to serve everyone, because in everyone we serve God. . . ."

"Like St. Paul: being free, make oneself the slave of all so as to win over as many as possible to Christ."[2]

"Persons who want to be a channel for unity must maintain themselves constantly in an abyss of humility so that they lose their own soul for the benefit and service of God in their neighbor."

"They only re-enter themselves in order to find God and pray for their brothers and for themselves."

"They constantly live as if 'cleansed out,' because they are totally 'in love with' the will of God. . . . And in love with their neighbor's will, whom they want to serve for the sake of God. A servant does nothing but what his Master orders."

The next thought affords one a glimpse of what a great revolution this ideal can effect:

"If all people, or at least a group, however small, were really servants of God in their 'neighbor,' the world would soon belong to Christ." It says at the end of the note that if our neighbor is loved this way, mutual love (unity) is achieved, and the Testament of Jesus will be fulfilled.

It goes on to state more exactly who our neighbor is: it is the brother or sister who comes our way at each moment of our day. He or she has got to be loved in a way that will induce the birth, growth, and development of Christ in him or her.

"It's important to have a unique concept of who is our 'neighbor.'

"Our neighbor is the brother who passes our way at this present moment in our life. Be ever ready to be of service to him, because in him we serve God. To have a simple eye means to see only one Father, to serve God in our neighbor; to have only one brother: Jesus.

"The simple eye recognizes 'a Christ coming to be' " in everyone. The person with a simple eye puts himself at everyone's service. . . so that Christ may come and may grow in them. In each it sees a Christ being born, who must grow, live, doing good—as a new child of God—, must die and rise and be glorified. . . .

"We can give ourselves no peace until—through our continual service—we discover in our neighbor the spiritual face of Christ.

"In this way, we live Christ. . . and serve Christ in our neighbor so that He may grow in age and wisdom and grace. . . .

"That's why we will fulfil our Ideal (Jesus' only ideal): 'Ut omnes unum sint' ('That they may all be one') when we make the best of the moment in the neighbor's service. . . ."

So our ideal is to bring about what Jesus prayed for on the evening of Maundy Thursday, when—having instituted the Eucharist and the Priesthood and given His disciples the New Commandment—He descended (as the tradition has it) an open stairway towards the torrent of Cedron: "That they may all be one."[3]

All one. As long as all are not one, those "all" that Jesus surely had in mind, the Focolare cannot rest. That is the goal for which we were born, the purpose for which He raised us up.

No other motives or goals were present to our minds, not at that stage.

Way far from our minds, for example, was the idea of ecumenism, of which we were absolutely ignorant. A few years later, around the year 1950, when visiting the Jesuit Father Boyer, founder of the "Foyer Unitas," I was asked the question if unity, as we conceived of it, was in function of the unity of the Church? I answered definitely in the negative. God had not yet unveiled His plans for us in that sense.

Unity. What does it mean? In that same note from 1946 we find some explanation, still expressed in terms we had learned at school: "We mustn't make a mixture, but a combination, and this will only come about if each person loses himself in the heat of the flame of divine love.

"What is left if two or more (persons) 'combine'? Jesus—the One.

". . .When the union passes away, it leaves only one trace: Christ."

In a letter of 1947 we find a definition of unity, given on the basis of our experience: "Ah! Unity, unity! What divine beauty! We have no human words to express it! It's Jesus!"

In a letter later on, in 1948, we read again: ". . .Unity! Who would risk speaking about it? It is as indescribable as God Himself! You feel it, you see it, you enjoy it, but. . . it is indescribable! All enjoy it when it is present, all suffer when it is absent. It is peace, joy, love, ardor, the climate of heroism and the greatest generosity. It is Jesus in our midst!"

So, unity is Jesus.

Yes, unity is Jesus. When He rose, He said: "Know that I am with you always, until the end of the world!"[4] Unity is one of the ways He is present in the Church, besides the Eucharist, His Word, and His presence in those whose duty it is to evangelize or guide the community, and His presence in the poor... in whom He lies concealed.

We have been called to live unity at every moment of our daily lives. We sensed that this could be done by being of help to our brothers and sisters. But then, how can we manage to do this best? Ever since the first years it has been evident to us that a good way is to "make ourselves one" with every neighbor we run into.

It often happens, and still does, that one gets caught up in his work, in a hurry, even in a wish to do God's will, and we slip into what seems to us His will, when we are really mistaken. What God wants of us more than anything else is that we make ourselves one with the person beside us, with the one who walks with us through life, with whoever we get to know day by day, even if—as can happen—it is through the media: television, radio, newspapers... most of all with people who are suffering and people deprived of God.

One of our notes from 1946 says: "...We ought to be one with our brother, not in an idealized way, but in a real way. Not in a future way but in the present.

"Being one means feeling in ourselves what our neighbors feel. Deal with their feelings as if they were our own, making them our own through out concern. *Be them*, doing this for the love of... Jesus in our neighbor.

"To be able to love our neighbors, we've got to undo the strings around this hard and stony heart of ours, and get a heart of flesh."

When God, in those beginning years, was teaching us how to live the way He planned for us, we spent a lot of time training ourselves in the practice of "making ourselves one" with other people.

It's no easy thing. We have to be empty in ourselves: chase our own ideas out of our heads, our own affections out of our hearts, everything out of our wills, to identify ourselves with the other person.

When I'm talking to someone who would like to be part of the Focolare and take me into his confidence, although an instant reply wants to burst out, I take a lot of time to relegate all my own ideas, until the other has poured out the full contents of his heart into mine. I'm convinced—also because experience has taught me—that when I do this, at the end the Holy Spirit suggests exactly what I ought to say. In fact, by making myself empty I am loving, and He manifests Himself if I love.⁵ Thousands of times I have tested this and found that had I interrupted the speech half way through, I would have said something which was not right, something unenlightened, something merely "human." Whereas, if my love lets the speaker unburden his mind into mine, I am then able to give a complete answer.

If this method of love manages to get established between two people, this way of mutual compenetration, then the union is made which brings Christ into our midst.

If we have been called to unity, the way to God, for us, passes through our neighbor. It is through this passage, which may sometimes be as dim and dark as a tunnel, that one comes to the light. This is the mysterious path God asks us to take in order to get to Him.

He wants us every day and every hour to perfect this art, a tiring one at times and exhausting, but always wonderful too, vital and fertile, the art of "making ourselves one" with other people: the art of loving.

It is the cross we've got to nail ourselves to from day to day: a cross which is pre-eminently ours. For us, and for the people we love, it's our life, and if it is mutual, it is Life itself come among us. It is Jesus.

The Ideal of our life has been God from the start. He descended and is descending to live in our midst by means of unity, because "Where there is charity and love, there is God"[6] and "Where two or three are gathered in my name, there am I in their midst."[7] Our way of finding God is in unity. That is the principal place where a *focolarino,* and whoever else chooses this road, finds Him. And only if we find Him there do we have the grace to find Him fully in the Eucharist, in the Word, in the Hierarchy. . . because He gives us lights on all of these supernatural realities.

It is a wonderful thing, which we still find astounding, to see how, from the time when the Focolare was first finding its legs, Jesus was stimulating us to emphasize so strongly this phrase from St. Peter: "Above all, let your love for one another be constant. . . ."[8]

Yes, because that is the novelty of the good news: above all, mutual and continual charity. Love as the foundation for the whole edifice, the soul of the whole life, the only thing which can give value to the whole.

In a letter of 1948, addressed to a group of religious who understood God's gift to the Focolare and took it to themselves, was written: "above all (even if this 'all' included very good and sacred things, such as prayer, or the celebration of the holy Mass, etc.) be one! Then it won't any longer be you working, praying, or celebrating, but Jesus in you always."

Unity must be preserved at all costs. It costs indeed our death, but produces this life which is Jesus. And this is the life, a victory over—and reward for—our death, which gives the world life through the Communion of Saints, and through the witness it offers, and through the strength it gives to face the world and all its disunity, offering it a cure.

"Brothers," says another letter also of 1948, "let everything else go, but unity never! Where there is unity there is Jesus. . . . Don't be afraid to die. You've learned already by experience that unity requires all to die, to give life to the One. Let your death bring Life to life. This Life which brings many other souls to life without your knowing it. Jesus said this Himself: 'for *their* sakes I sanctify myself.'[9] To bring unity to your city and to the world, be one among yourselves. This is the only way. That unity, in which Love is alive, will give you the strength to face every type of disunity outside and to fill every void. . . ."

In another place it is written: "I would prefer to let the whole world go to pieces, so long as He is always with us. . . . Brothers, our Lord has given us an ideal. . . . Let us stick to it faithfully, at whatever cost, even if some day our souls might have to cry out in the torment of infinite pain: 'My God, my God, why have even You forsaken me?'. . . If we stick faithfully to our commitment (that they may be one) the world will see unity. . . . All will be one, if we will be one!

"And don't be afraid to give up everything for unity; unless we love. . . beyond all measure, unless we lose our own judgment and our own desires, we shall never be one! Wise is the one who dies so that God may live in him! And unity is the field of battle for these fighters for true life against the false life. . . . Unity above all! Arguments don't count for much, nor do the holiest of discussions, unless we give life to Jesus among us. . . ."

Just as mutual love is a commandment for Christians, so unity is the foremost of our duties. The *focolarini's* Rule make unity the norm of all norms: the first of them all is to have Jesus in our midst. This duty brings with it, however, a new joy, a joy that is full, the joy promised by Jesus with the words: ". . . in order that they may possess the fullness of my joy."[10]

Joy, one of God's gifts to unity, is an asset to which we may not be paying sufficient attention. In our physical nature we don't usually feel health, but we notice pain.

It is the same with joy in our supernatural life, which may be the reason why it doesn't get the notice it deserves. All the same, it is an extraordinary gift, and very highly prized.

If we look at the world that surrounds us: all its apathy, all its boredom, all its sorrow, and how much thirst, how much madness for happiness. What does the phenomenon of drugs mean, the drunkenness of cinema, of television, and the rebellions in the world? Even the wars? They express a thirst for peace and justice and happiness. The human heart was made for joy. All right, God revealed to the first Christians, and even today to us, the source where joy may be mined.

Because the *focolarini* live on unity, they are happy. Because the *focolarini* bring unity, they are a dispenser of joy.

We've always said that joy is a *focolarino's* uniform; and the gift that the *focolarino* owes to the world is happiness.

Others are called to provide food or lodging or counsel or instruction or housing. . . .

The gift of the *focolarini* is joy, along with, or without, all those other gifts, depending on whether or not "making themselves one" with their neighbor demands that they give them food, or drink, find them work, pay them a visit, bear with them, or simply share.

In any case, we are called to give comfort, bring peace, light, and above all joy, to make the world smile.

In the first days of our life this new joy made us jubilant, we wanted to share it with everyone and we felt grateful to God for having given it to us.

I wrote in a letter, speaking to Jesus: ". . .The happiness that we feel in unity, which You have given us through Your death, is something we want to give all the souls that touch ours. We cannot reserve it to ourselves, seeing that there are so many. . . who feel hunger and thirst for this complete peace, this boundless joy. . . . Our heart is bursting,. . . our very selves, in order that You alone may live in us. . . . We have chosen You on the cross, in Your most forsaken state, to be our all, and You have then given us paradise on earth. You are God, God, God."

We have to thank God for this joy, although we must not become attached to it, but turn it into a springboard from which to bring unity into the world.

"Do this (preserve unity)," I wrote in 1948, as a sacrosanct *duty,* despite the fact that it will bring you an immense joy.

"Jesus promised the fullness of joy to those who live unity. . . .

"Enjoy your unity, but for the Lord's sake, not for your own. . . .

"Let's make unity among ourselves the starting-gate from which we run . . . to where there is no unity, in order to bring it there.

"And more: as Jesus preferred the cross for Himself rather than Mt. Tabor, so let us too prefer to stay with the person who is not in unity, so that we can suffer with him or her and then be certain that our love is pure. . . ."

Unity means making ourselves one with our neighbors.

But suppose there were no neighbors around? Suppose we had to be by ourselves at work or rest or relaxation or study?

We know the answer: being completely submerged in the will of God for the present time, the unique will of God which varies in each person's case, all together we become the will of God. And, since God and the will of God are identical, this is how we live our being-God-by-participation: thereby we are one with Him and with each other.

I recall that from 1947 on, a method we used for having unity was precisely the fulfilment of God's will, to express our love for Him concretely.

A letter to the first women in the Focolare says:

"Get just one idea fixed in your heads. It was always one idea that produced great saints. And our idea is this: unity. (Union with God): 'Yes, Father!'

"At each present moment, let us repeat 'Yes, Father,' to His will. Yes, yes, yes, always and only yes. This will make you share in our unity, which is found only in God.

"His will is the bond between us and consumes us in Him and in each other. . . .

"Unity means I will what He wills. . . .

"Unity: continual direct communion with God with the radical mortification of all that is not God in the present moment. I want nothing but God. . . . Unity: among ourselves, in this stupendous communion of souls all over the world, shut in and secured behind nothing but the love of God."

So our ideal is unity and nothing else. And this has got to be emphasized even today, in fact today a lot more than at our beginnings. In those days, under the impulse of the Holy Spirit, it was perfectly clear. It is quite evident now to the *focolarini* and the other members of the Focolare. It goes without saying that we have unity in our Focolare households and likewise, I trust, in the "nuclei" of the Volunteers, the Gen units and so on. But in the Focolare at large? Among all our other friends?

Is there not a danger that in certain places our Movement may appear to be a movement for the living and diffusion of the Word of Life,* rather than a movement for unity?

To live the Word is surely an excellent thing, but this practice too has to happen within the reality of unity. Unity has to come first.

If we believe that we can sum up our Ideal as "the choice of God," we are wrong, because that is something present in every spirituality, practised by St. Francis, St. Catherine, St. Dominic, St. Ignatius and all the saints.

If we think our spirituality focuses on "the will of God," we have missed the point again. All the saints have "willed" the will of God.

If we affirm that we must walk along the path of love, we have still not picked out what makes our spirituality

---

* It is common knowledge that it has been a custom in the Movement of the Focolari, from the time it started in 1943-45, to pick out some phrase from the Gospel with the intention that it be applied to one's daily life for a set period of time (a month, as a rule) for the re-evangelization of life. With this in view, the magazine "Living City" publishes a commentary, composed by Chiara Lubich, on this same Word of Life, which gets reprinted and diffused in what is, given the extensive development of the Movement, a very considerable number of copies, both in Italy and abroad. Allusion is made to this in the text. (Cf. also Chiara Lubich, *Scritti Spirituali* vol. 3, Rome 1979, pp. 121-158).

different. Other spiritualities emphasize the same New Commandment; consequently it is inadequate to define our vocation.

We have to choose God in the way He wants to be chosen, love Him in other words by concretely realizing His Testament. We must do His will, which in our case means unity; love, by "making ourselves one" with our neighbor; love one another to the point of being perfected in one. We must embrace Jesus Forsaken who is, as we shall see further on, the key to unity and has therefore always to be loved with unity in view. Live the Word of Life, having laid first the foundation of continuous mutual love for each other, living the Word as further nourishment for that love.

To live the Word represented of course, at that time, a certain novelty, but it was more the communing about the experiences it gave us (for our evangelization and sanctification) that characterized the Focolare.

And so the Word too must serve unity, because unity stands at the summit of the thought of Christ, synthesizing and summarizing His commandments. This is what Jesus always had us understand. What God wants most of all of us, as the Movement of the Focolari,—which at one time was also called the Movement of Unity—, is that we give rise to living cells all over the place, increasingly fervent, with Christ in their midst; more and more of them, so that we set fires far and wide in families, offices, factories, schools, parishes, monasteries, to feed a conflagration of the love of God in the Church and in society. It's not for nothing that they call us *"focolarini"* (people of fire) and our homes *"focolari"* (fireplaces). Only by living in this way can we be certain of being on the right track. Even though in some places or nations we may be only a "little flock," we are still authentic, belonging to Him, and oriented to the "ut omnes" ("That they may all be one").

This is the only adjustment or readjustment that we need in order to be able to hope for all of God's blessings.

For the rest, God's agenda for the Focolare has been this from the outset: reach out to one's own environment, perfecting one's own neighbors in unity while maintaining openness to all others.

"Your first responsibility," so says again one of the letters already quoted, "is to see to it that all of your confreres be one, without excluding other neighbors whom God places near you. Die... completely in the Jesus among you! Have everything in common... then Jesus will perfect your brothers, one by one, who live alongside you, and will prepare those afar off for unity. Just as every object which floats by a whirlpool in the sea or in a lake is irreparably drawn by the vortex (a whirlpool is formed by the meeting of two currents... Isn't this too a symbol of unity?), so every person who meets Jesus (Jesus among us) will be lost in His love irretrievably. My hope is that Jesus among you will cast His nets into the wide world of your Order and that the daily catch will be miraculous."

On earth we live as part of the Church militant. We can't wage war without weaponry, or without an objective. The weapon is Christ alive in the most perfect unity between us. The objective is: "that they may all be one."

We cannot fail to see every person we encounter on the street as a candidate for unity. God certainly wants to see that person perfected in the Church in unity with his or her sisters and brothers. This is Jesus' dream.

JESUS FORSAKEN;
KEY TO UNION WITH GOD

I

In the preceding pages, we have begun a study of that characteristic pivot of our spirituality which is *unity*, picking up the first rays of this divine idea at its appearance at the start of the Focolare. It gave us the joyful and exciting conviction that, when we fulfill our specific vocation, unity being what God wants of us, the Risen One is alive among us, in the midst of the world where we are living.

Throughout this period of time, as a result, we have committed ourselves to kindling that divine presence among all who take part in our gatherings, at our various meetings, in every kind of society, often reminding ourselves of the original counsels received from the Holy Spirit, those ideas which first occupied our thoughts for the realization of unity.

This profound experience of unity was such a gift to us, such an important centering on the special charism of the Focolare, that it triggered a communal conversion, like a sort of death and resurrection, and we can certainly not make progress without continuing to do our full part to deserve the abiding presence of the Risen Jesus in our midst.

We would have liked now to go straight into a complete survey of our history, to see how this idea of unity has formed the background, the framework, and the goal of our entire journey; how it has animated all of our spirituality, our life forms, the discipline of our Work, its various structures, the very vows of the consecrated persons within it; how it poses itself as the general and specific purpose of the Focolare. But as we see it, it would not be good to release ourselves from what we feel as demands of the Holy Spirit, who, if He has announced unity to us, from the beginning, as the characterisic of our spiritual path, has also revealed, even from that time, the key to its achievement.

We have in fact felt the urgency not only of a legitimate desire, but also of the Church's guidance—which, to safeguard the authenticity of their inspiration, invites religious families and movements to refashion themselves in conformity to the times when the Holy Spirit brought them to birth. When we look back to the beginnings of the Focolare, we see that, even before we had acquired ideas about the way to realize unity, a model was proposed to us, a figure, a life: that of Him who was able to truly "make Himself one" with all the human beings who have lived in the past, live now in the present, and will live in the future; He effected unity, paying for it by the cross, with His blood and His cry; He who has given His presence to the Church as the Risen One for all time, until the end of the world: Jesus Crucified and Forsaken.

His reality, and our understanding of Him, preceded, even in time, every other consideration. If we are right to keep the 7th of December, 1943 (the date of my consecration to God) as the beginning of our story, we have to remember that on the 24th of January, 1944, Jesus Forsaken had already presented Himself to our mind and to our heart.

But let us proceed in proper order.

As we have done for "unity," so too for Jesus Forsaken, to recall the first thoughts we had about Him we will look to the remembrance of episodes and circumstances, and to the reading of the notes we have kept. They are familiar events and thoughts, but we need even today to pass them in review, for the sake of a more complete analysis of this theme.

A first episode was the encounter with Jesus Forsaken at Dori's * house, an encounter which this time we will let her describe herself.

She tells: "We went in search of the poor and it was probably from them that I caught an infection on my face. I was covered with sores and the medicines did not halt the disease. But, with my face appropriately protected, I kept on going to Mass and to our Saturday meetings. . . .

"It was cold, and to go outside under such conditions could be bad for me. Since my family would not let me go out, Chiara asked a Capuchin priest to bring me Communion. While I was making my thanksgiving, the priest asked Chiara what was, in her opinion, the moment of Jesus' greatest suffering during His passion.

* Dori Zamboni, one of the first women in the movement.

She replied she had always heard that it was the pain He felt in the Garden of Olives. Then the priest remarked: 'But I believe, rather, it was what He felt on the cross, when He cried out: "My God, my God, why have you forsaken me?"'[12]

"As soon as the Father had left, having heard Chiara's words, I turned to her, feeling sure of some explanation. Instead, she said: 'If Jesus' greatest pain was His abandonment by His Father, we will choose Him as our Ideal and that is the way we will follow Him.'

"At that moment, in my mind, in my imagination, the conviction impressed itself that for us our ideal was the Jesus of the contorted face crying out to the Father. And my poor facial sores, which I saw as shadows of His pain, were a joy to me, because they made me resemble Him a little. From that day on, Chiara spoke to me often, in fact constantly, of Jesus Forsaken. He was *the* living personality in our lives."

Let's go on to a second episode, and another of our practices of those early days.

As I have said at other times, the various aspects of the new life springing up in us often arose out of a concrete step. The practice of what we called "making a stack," heaping our few poor articles of clothing together, was the simple way we started living poverty and the use of our goods.

"Putting our books away in the attic" was the beginning of a new kind of knowledge.

We eliminated from our vocabulary the word (misunderstood in those days) "apostolate." This turned into a source of radiation for a rediscovered love of God.

46

The writing of a letter of invitation, out of sheer obedience, to forty-odd people we had never met—following a method we thought artificial, a model of "non-relationship"—, was the premise to that broadening flood of short letters which became the initial bond between people in the nascent movement.

Again, the elimination of all furniture from our little house, keeping nothing but mattresses for sleeping on the floor, was the beginning of a new style of interior decorating, simple and harmonious, and became simultaneously the first outward manifestation of our typical spiritual life. At that time, we hung one single object on the wall: a picture portraying Jesus Forsaken, to bring home to us that He alone had to be the treasure of our existence. Each morning when we woke up, we formulated this decision in a brief prayer: 'Because You were forsaken...', to which we added, as we turned to Mary: "because you were desolate...."

This stood for a unique, radical choice: Jesus Forsaken.

Our letters at that time used to underline this: "Forget everything... even the sublimest things; let yourself be ruled by a single Idea, by one God, who must penetrate every fiber of your being: Jesus Crucified" (7.21.45).

"Are you familiar with the lives of the saints?... They were a single word: Jesus Crucified;... Christ's wounds were their resting-place; Christ's blood was the health-giving bath of their soul; the wound in Christ's side was the casket that they filled with their love.

"Ask of Jesus Crucified, in the name of His heart-rending cry, a passion for His passion.

47

"...He must be everything for you" (7.21.45).

Jesus Forsaken was the only book we wanted to read.

"Yes, true enough, I'm going to college, but there isn't any book, no matter how beautiful and profound, that gives my soul such strength and above all so much love as Jesus Crucified. ..." (6.7.44).

And again:

"But above all, take instruction from one book... Jesus Crucified, who was abandoned by everybody. He who cries out:

'My God, my God, why have you forsaken me?' Oh! if that divine face, contorted in agony, those reddened eyes, which still look on you with kindness, forgetting my sins and yours, which reduced Him to this, could be always before your gaze! ..." (1.30.44).

This radical choice was renewed from time to time in the years that followed.

A letter of 1948 says:

"Forget everything in life: office, work, people, responsibilities, hunger, thirst, rest, even your own soul... in order to possess nobody else but Him! This is everything... to love the way He loved us, even to the point of feeling forsaken by His Father for our sake" (8.14.48).

And in 1949: "I have only one Spouse on earth, Jesus Forsaken. I have no other God but Him." And so we knew nobody else but Him. We had no desire to know anyone else. The Holy Spirit said to us over and over: "I know nothing but Christ, and Him crucified." Love for Him was exclusive: it permitted no compromises.

The choice of God, which was characteristic of the first step we took in our new way of life, became more specific: for us, to choose God meant to choose Jesus Forsaken.

And here we must pause.

When we revive our ideas, and remember our first intuitions, we feel a need to give the right direction to the Focolare in whatever corner of the earth it is found (it has to be a movement for unity, and not just a movement, for instance, for the better living of God's Word). So also, when we get back to our first inspirations, we are aware of the need to emphasize that our choices cannot be two: the choice of God and the further choice of Jesus Forsaken; the choice for us is a single one: God in Jesus Forsaken. The God of Love we chose lives in Him, God's will for us lives in Him, in Him is contained the possibility of actualizing the New Commandment, the measure or degree of love that He is asking from us. He is, *par excellence* , the Word Jesus has sown in the world when He planted the Focolare.

The actual living of Jesus Forsaken gives us the possibility, the sole possibility, of having with us Jesus Himself. It is by loving Him that we shall be able to be "another Mary." By loving Him we will work effectively for the realization of His last testament. With Him we will be really living the Church. Through our love for Him we will make room in our hearts, and in those of many others, for the Holy Spirit.

That is something which needs to be made clear.

It is only through love for Jesus Forsaken that we'll be able to avoid making mistakes, for example, in relationships forming between new members when they are just starting out on this spiritual way, mistakes due to a too human interpretation of the love required by the Ideal of the God of Love.

In fact, because one is at a stage when the idea is not yet very clear, due to his inexperience one can think of love for God, and love for neighbor, and mutual love, and practise them,mostly as an effusion of sentiment.

As we know, even Jesus' heart certainly felt special palpitations; but the principal way He manifested His love was by self-sacrifice on the cross, forsaken.

Jesus Forsaken is our style of love. He has taught us to annihilate everything inside us and around us, to "make ourselves one" with God; He teaches us to stifle our thoughts and attachments, to mortify our senses, to drop even our own inspirations so that we can "make ourselves one" with our neighbor's, which means to serve them, to love them.

The radicalness that characterized our first choice of Jesus Forsaken, the decision to see nothing else, strikes us even today as a message, a specific and urgent invitation to renew our choice of Him as the only love of our life; it comes to us like an admonition not only to embrace all the pain that comes like a meeting with a beloved Spouse, expected and consequently welcomed always, immediately, and joyfully *, but to look at Him as the gauge of our love for our neighbor: a measureless

* This is a reference to a spiritual attitude adopted in the Movement, which relates to the Christian way of taking up our cross.

measure within our duty to give our all, reserving nothing for ourselves, not even what seem to be the most spiritual values, even the most divine; to imitate His manner of loving, even to the heroic practice of all the virtues included in love.

We have to face this question: have we truly loved *Him alone* today in our heart? Or have other things taken His place, even if only for short periods of time, like our own ego, or other people, or activities, jobs, studies or objects, around which we have got to live in order to fulfill God's will?

Jesus Forsaken was the only book we took to read. And what did the Holy Spirit let us read in this book?

What we saw in Him was *the summit of His love because it was the summit of His pain*. In fact, Jesus Forsaken reveals *all* the love of a God.

A letter of January 1944 (one week after our first encounter with Jesus Forsaken) already states:

"You'll be the recipient of joys, you'll be the recipient of pain and of anguish... if you will make an effort to see Jesus, in the way I have presented Him to you, as I always present Him to you, at the culmination of His pain, which is the culmination of His love..." (1.30.44).

And elsewhere:

"...that's where it all is. It is the total love of a God." (6.7.44).

And again:

"Do you realize He has given us *everything*? What more could have been given us by a God who, for love, seems to have forgotten that He *is* God?" (12.8.44).

So from the beginning, with no limit to our thankfulness, we have been aware of the superb gift in our call to follow Him:

"You don't know how lucky you and we are, to be able to follow this Forsaken Love.

"It is His inscrutable plan to have chosen us from among many thousands, to let us hear His anguished cry: 'My God, my God, why have you forsaken me?'" (12.8.44).

When we take these writings now and look them over, we get a feeling that this love for Jesus Forsaken entered in, and penetrated, and exploded in our heart, a fire which consumes everything, leaving behind nothing, a sort of divine passion which gets heart, mind, and strength so involved that it sweeps them away, like lightning illuminating everything. We saw something. We understood. It meant rivers of light to us.

Jesus Forsaken illuminated, for example, the place pain occupies in the divine economy. "Jesus converted the world by His word, by His example, by His preaching; but He transformed the world by the cross which was the way He proved His love." (1944).

What was perceived in Him and His immense pain was the unfurling of His love. This vision set our hearts on fire. And it stimulated us to value our own pain, as an expression of our love for Him, and to become co-redeemers in Him and with Him.

"Think of this, . . . the Lord came to the world just once, and came as a man, and let Himself be nailed to a cross. This thought gives me the strength to accept joyfully the little cross that we always carry with us" (1944).

"A person who knows what Love is and unites his own pains to those of Jesus on the cross, letting his own drop of blood fall into the sea of the divine blood of the Christ, has the highest place of honor that a human being can reach: he has become like God, when He the redeemer of the world came to earth. . ." (1944).

"Believe it, a minute of your life in the white sheets of that bed is worth more, if you can accept God's gift joyfully. . . than all the work of a preacher who talks and talks with a little love for the Lord" (1944). "He has poured a great passion into my heart: a passion for Himself crucified and abandoned.

"He who has told me—from the height of His cross: '. . . I have given up everything that was mine. . . everything. I am not beautiful any more; I am no longer strong; I have no peace here; up here, justice is dead; I am ignorant of science; what was truth for me has vanished. All I have left is my Love, this love that wanted *for your sake* to dump all the riches I possessed *as God. . .*'

"As I hear those words, He seems to be calling me. . . to follow Him. . . . He is the real Passion of my life." (12.25.44).

All pain seems like nothing before Him. I look forward to every pain, great or small, as God's best gift. For it is the test and proof of my own love for Him!" (6.7.44).

The culmination of love was not the only thing we saw in Jesus Forsaken. The place of suffering in the divine economy was not the only thing He revealed to us. In Him we seemed to gaze upon the secret of sanctity. "Remember Saint Rita. In the dark and dim background of her little room, where her two children slept, was the crucified God-Man. He was the secret of her love. He, and He alone.

"Shining down from that crucifix she saw the perfect example of patience, forgiveness, a tenacious, unshaken love which could hold out even till death, even to dying forsaken and abandoned.

"He was her Guide along the steepest paths of sanctity, because Jesus Crucified was Rita's first love . . ." (1948).

Because He revealed all these riches, we felt He was the pearl of great price that God was offering us. His sort of love was so exalted, so extraordinary (it had reduced Him to a "worm of the earth!," to "sin," for our sakes), that we were convinced no one could ever have resisted Him. He is worth so very much, that there could be no fair exchange.

"We have found it! We have discovered the pearl of great price.

"Oh, what Love we feel!

"That man, that 'worm of the earth!'. . . He belongs to us.

"Any soul that finds Him leaves everything for His embrace. She too, like the Bride in the Canticle, goes in search of her treasure, loves Him, and worships Him!

"Won't the love of such a lover attract all others to itself? I wish I could run through the whole world and collect other hearts for Him! I feel there are not enough hearts in the whole world to equal a Love as large as God." (6.15.48).

Finally, a very special light.

Our experience was still in its first year when the Spirit was already showing us Jesus Forsaken as the model of a new way of life. A note in 1944 said:

"As God, He made that cry the model of a new life, a new sort of ideal" (12.8.44).

So this was a new spirituality which the Spirit was pouring out upon the world. We were the first for Him to call to this new ideal.

In the course of time it was becoming clearer and clearer: God is calling us to Unity (we have spelled out above what were the signs of this call), and Jesus Forsaken is its secret; for the fulfilment of the Testament of Jesus "that all may be one," He must come first.

In a letter of 1948, written to young religious, we described the experience we had had. We attested, with some surprise, to an existing connection between Jesus Forsaken and unity: unity with God and unity between people.

"In my experience, only the strength of a Love-Pain as powerful as that of Jesus Forsaken can keep a soul on his feet when he finds himself on the front lines in the cause of unity." (4.1.48).

"This is the reason, brothers, why... we have taken as our goal in life, our only purpose, our everything: Jesus Crucified and crying out: 'My God, my God, why have you forsaken me?' This means Jesus in His deepest pain, suffering infinite disunity... in order to give us perfect unity, which we will reach in an absolute sense in Paradise, but only in a relative sense here below. . ." (4.1.48).

In another letter to a religious:

"Try. . . to embrace Him.

"If I had not had Him with me in the trials of life, this way of unity would never have happened, unless it had been Jesus' will to raise it up somewhere else in a similar way.

"Christ Forsaken won every battle in me, terrible battles.

"But you have got to be crazy with His love, a love which synthesizes all the pains of soul and body: He is medicine. . . for every kind of soul-pain. . ." (4.23.48).

And so, Jesus Forsaken is the key to the charism, the secret to unity. With Him one will always keep moving ahead. We will need to keep this in mind for the future, against those difficult times which may come, and indeed will have to, when we may be seized with doubts whether things are going to keep on progressing as in the past. In these moments it will be good to remind oneself of this initial light, this truly extraordinary experience.

II

We concluded the first meditation on Jesus Forsaken with an attempt to understand all that we contemplated in Him after His first appearance.

Let us now read, almost in its entirety, a letter written to a Gen-Re * in 1948. The motto of the letter was: "My

God, my God, why have even You abandoned me?"
It already contains, as we can see, the most important
pronouncements about Jesus Forsaken. There they
exploded with their full force and clarity. This page is
a small synthesis of our doctrine about Him.

Its opening words assert right away that unity is
truly understood by anyone who loves Jesus Forsaken:

". . . I am convinced that in its most spiritual aspect,
at its deepest and most intimate level, unity can be
understood only by a person who has chosen as her por-
tion of life. . . Jesus Forsaken, crying out 'My God, my
God, why have you forsaken me?'" (3.30.48).

Jesus Forsaken is proclaimed as the secret and
guarantee of unity.

"Brother, now that I have found that you understand
this secret of unity, I would like to talk to you about
it forever, and I could. Try to understand that Jesus
Forsaken is everything. He is the guarantee of unity.
Every light we have received on unity pours out from
that cry" (3.30.48).

We affirm that to choose Him is snynonymous with
giving birth to an infinite number of souls for unity.

"To choose Him as our only goal, only objective, the
point of arrival for our own life is. . . to generate an
infinite number of souls into unity. . ." (3.30.48).

* Gen-Re. The Gen are the young people living by the
spirituality of the Focolare (Gen Movement - New Generation
Movement). When they are members of a religious family (order),
we call them Gen-Re.

In continuation, this letter states categorically that from now on this nascent spirituality will hinge on two things: Unity and Jesus Forsaken; they are—it says—like two faces of the same medal.

"The book of light *, which the Lord is writing in my soul has two aspects: one page shines with a mysterious love: Unity. Another page shines with a mysterious pain: Jesus Forsaken. They are two sides to one and the same medal" (3.30.48).

Of course, this light is a new one, and it has to be protected so that "holy things" are not given to people who are not ready for them.

"Brother, not everyone understands these words. Let's not give them to just anyone. Let Forsaken Love see itself surrounded only by hearts who understand Him, because they have felt Him come into their lives and have found in Him the solution to every problem..." (3.30.48).

During that period of time, Jesus Forsaken was defined as "the great amputation," who seemed unwanted both on earth and in Heaven. We used to say the world doesn't want Him, not even Heaven wants Him; therefore we can have Him, all for our own.

Because He had been uprooted from both earth and Heaven, He brought into unity those who were cut off,

---

* in other words, the fundamental inspiration of the Focolare: its spirituality of unity, whose key is Jesus Forsaken (cf. Rule: Chapter 10 and John Paul II to the priests and religious of the Focolare on 4.30.82, reported in the "Osservatore Romano" of 5.1.82).

the people who had been uprooted from God. By golly, this was the only way to unity!

The truth is that for Jesus the way to win is to lose, the way to life is to die; the grain of wheat has to die to be able to produce the ear of grain; a tree must be trimmed if it's to bear good fruit. That is His law; one of His paradoxes. The Holy Spirit was making us understand that in order to bring about the "*ut omnes** " in the world, we would have to bring the abandonment to perfection in ourselves, and receive Jesus Forsaken, in the absence of unity.

This letter was written in 1949 to a few religious brothers whose superiors had not given them permission to participate in such a novel movement:

"Is it not understood yet... that the greatest Ideal a human heart can yearn after—unity—is a pipe-dream and a mirage, if he who wants it does not set his heart exclusively upon Jesus abandoned by all, even by His Father? This apparent severance (of yours)... from your brothers and sisters outside your college, who are fighting, living, and suffering for your own Ideal, isn't this, perhaps, a little piece of Jesus Forsaken for you?...

"There is only one way that you will form yourselves for unity, and that is on the strength of embracing with all your heart Jesus Forsaken, an injury to your body and a darkness to your soul.... There lies the greatest secret and final dream of our Jesus: 'That they may all be one!' Both you and we, as we share in this infinite Pain, will

* "that they all may be one"

make an effective contribution to the unity of all the brethren!" (2.17.49).

When we read these early writings we catch on to what this God-given charism was all about: the *"ut omnes"*. And to reach that destination there was a road, a key, and a secret: Jesus Forsaken.

Jesus came into the world in order that all might be one. Jesus on the cross and abandoned paid for this goal. He wants a helping hand to reach it: the Work of Mary has made this its special purpose. With Jesus Forsaken, in Him and through Him, it can be accomplished.

The charism of the Focolare descended from Heaven with the precise intention of the Holy Spirit to work for Jesus' cause, which the Church has always made its own: "That all may be one." Whoever those little letters were written to, in those early years, they all asked one thing: dedicate yourself to the *"ut omnes"*. It is symptomatic that the first addressees were girls, and men-religious, young folks and adults: this meant that for an ideal which made it its business to be concerned with all people, every vocation was mobilized.

Some people understood, some didn't. But whoever was touched and illuminated by it, felt a moral commitment to the *"ut omnes"*.

This love for Jesus Forsaken entered into us like fire, and naturally stimulated us to look for Him everywhere.

We felt we were in touch with Him, lonely and forsaken, dwelling through grace in the depths of many human hearts: "When you find yourself in front of a person, any at all, remember that in that heart lives God, God who might be abandoned by that same heart.... Who on earth ever remembers, in fact, that he has Jesus at the center of his heart?" (undated).

We used to find Him in our neighbor, because God's abandonment was the price paid for them.

"Oh,... give Him your whole existence! Give Him your will.... His will is all in this: that you love God with your whole heart! Love your neighbor as yourself. Your neighbor.... Love him... and think that his soul is worth the immense pain of Jesus Forsaken! Therefore love him as if he *were* Jesus Forsaken!" (1.11.45).

We found Him in persons abandoned to themselves because of the war. "I know that people here have been abandoned while everybody is escaping. But I do not choose to leave them. Jesus paid for them with His blood" (1.9.45).

We found Him in our young hearts' homesickness for our distant parents.

"I see Him there on the cross, Him too, suffering homesickness and the abandonment by his Father..." (12.25.44).

We found Him in tabernacle and on the cross. "I wish I could be with you, take you by the arm, and lead you to the little church on the hill, bring you near the tabernacle and show you two things. Down below a cold, barren tabernacle, surrounded perhaps with flowers and candles and the emptiness of hearts, and inside: the living Jesus! The Jesus who is God. He created you, and gave you the beauties of nature and the love in your heart.... The Jesus who—full of love for this human race (and for you and me within it)—has chosen, after that death, to perpetuate His painful abandonment in this tabernacle.... Then I would tell you to look up at Him in the crucifix. Has He loved you, or not? Tell me. And tell me what He must have felt when... He felt Himself forsaken by everybody, as He waited for death. In that painful situation not even His Father would look at Him." (1.11.45).

We found Him in the midst of sorrows and misunderstandings. "...never, never have we felt so keenly as we do today that the Lord has heard our prayers and truly loves us. We had not been aiming, of course, at the joys which flow naturally from the life of unity, but at the cross, and especially at a cry of pain issuing from the greatest pain there is: 'My God, my God, why have you forsaken me?'.... (One day it is our) Ideal taken for a kind of fanaticism or hysteria.... The finger of ridicule is pointed at us... (but) when all seems to fail, we see His divine Figure in agony branded upon our hearts, a unique pledge of the glory of the other world. O Heaven! up there, unity will be perfect" (7.7.47).

We found Him in the poor whom we sought out, in the sick to whom we paid visits, in prisoners, in people who had gone astray, for instance unmarried mothers....

We let our hearts be fanned by all the works of mercy that love can invent, different works to which the nascent Focolare would be called in each of its various branches. Just one name: Jesus Forsaken, has been given, is given, and will eventually be given, to everybody who has been, is, or will be blessed by this love.

In those early times, what was our attitude when faced with Jesus Forsaken?

We were struck most deeply by His love and we wanted absolutely to do something for Him. Not knowing at first what to do, we sought ways of manifesting our thankful love by offering Him consolation.

"Woe betide me if I were to hear you tell me that you have become lukewarm and no longer love Him who is everything for us! Isnt't it true that you have not forsaken Him?

"I have great hope of being able to console love with your two hearts. It would be torture if I were to see you fallen back into the life you led before—a good life all right, but without any love for God! Tell me it is not so. Reassure me. . ." (1.9.45).

It goes without saying that consoling Him means loving Him. "Look at Him on the cross, bled white, sending forth an atrocious cry. You know him well, because that cry is your life!: 'My God, my God, why have You forsaken me?', and He implies: 'Will you too abandon me?' And together with me you reply: 'Never, I would rather die.'

"My little sister, never abandoning love means: LOVE HIM, POSSESS LOVE!. . ."

Today people might think that the verb *to console*, which occurs frequently in these letters, and this stance to assume when faced with Jesus Forsaken, was something borrowed from popular piety, something picked up from some traditional spirituality with a touch of the medieval about it. It can indeed be said that Jesus, at the right hand of the Father in Heaven, has no need of our consolation.

But analyze these writings and we will understand their exact meaning.

If the historical Jesus at the moment of His abandonment seemed so alive and present to our heart, we never thought of Him except in connection with the Jesus who raised His cry of abandonment from His Mystical Body, in the humanity of that time, where He had real need of our help, our consolation.

"In such infinite pain Jesus needs our consolation. What is He missing in His anguished state?—God. How can we give Him God? If we are united among ourselves, we will have Him in our midst and the Jesus who will be born of our unity will console our Crucified Love! That is why we have got to make our unity grow in the amount of love and of souls! We want our king to grow to gigantic proportions among us. So we will go and try to mend every broken unity, all the more because in every broken or disconnected soul we hear the cry of our Jesus more or less loudly!..." (4.1.48)

Console Jesus Forsaken. We could say that it was now time to reap what He has sown, receiving the interest or dividends on what He has paid for.

Another way to love Him was to share His pain.

"This has been another day spent in loving although the 'evil birds' wanted to make it cruel and ugly. I left the bomb shelter after spending six hours down there. I wasn't cold, my heart was filled with Jesus Forsaken, for whose love I live suffering those discomforts that He grants me to endure, in the hope that He may be forsaken no longer..." (1.1.45)

We wanted to love Him by imitating Him. His abandonment stood for the absolutely limitless quality of His love. And so we felt that if we didn't take care even of seemingly insignificant things, we did not love as He loved.

"First and foremost Jesus wants my love. And I can arrive at loving Him His way by contemplating Him in His forsaken state: He has given Himself completely to me, and I've got to do the same, giving myself totally to Him. I cannot have my own will any longer; my will is His. My life will be to do His will with extreme faithfulness, even in little things; because otherwise I will have done nothing for Him..." (6.2.45) Since nothing but Him was chosen, we preferred Him to everything else.

"There are times when the will of God means pain, abandonment, and agony. To choose it as the soul's one 'preference' is to render indestructible our soul's unity with God and hence with our neighbor..." (4.23.48)

Console Him, share His pain, imitate Him, prefer Him: He was calling us to all that.

Let us now look at the effects of that behavioral attitude: new effects, never perhaps experienced before, at which we marveled.

The first effect was the distinct impression of finding ourselves on a supernatural level.

Let's read this letter from 1944:

"I am wedded to Him and I have tried to turn off every other desire for His sake... He and His cry at being forsaken have drawn me, Mama, and they've made me step over everything else, with a broken heart. Yes, . . . He alone could have done this. He who does not want us to make light of our (more sacred) affections, but makes us feel them in the very depth of our hearts and go beyond them . . ." (12.25.44).

Through this love for Jesus Forsaken we experienced Life, the supernatural life.

"Seek nothing but Him, long for nothing but Him; and when He comes close to your soul, embrace Him impetuously and find Life in Him! . . ." (4.23.48).

Love for Jesus Forsaken was developing virtues in our soul, starting from humility.

"You know how. . . in the innermost depths of my soul I bear the love for Him Forsaken and how I would love to turn His cry into my life, in the deepest humility. . . His cry is the fountain of all humility: In the final completion of His Divine Mission He is led by the Divine Will to cry of His abandonment by the Father who was perfectly one with Him . . ." (10.30.45).

Jesus Frosaken, when loved, brought the soul a gentle sweetness, rest, and fire:

"Don't (try to love Him) only when there is no alternative because we are being reminded of Him by our pain, . . . but prefer Him at *all* times; don't treasure your joys or the contentment you feel, even though they come through unity. . . but always ask to suffer with Him. He is honey to the soul, rest, and fire." (8.14.48)

He was consolation, companionship, fullness, serenity, love.

". . .You too. . .don't let yourself forget Jesus Forsaken. When everything in your life disappears, you'll refind Him, faithfully faithful: He who was betrayed in order to console everybody else who has been betrayed; a failure, to console every other who is a failure; a void, in order to fill up every other void; sad in order to cheer up every depression; the unloved who makes up— divinely—for every love lost or not found. Love Him in the inner chamber of your heart, which belongs, and always will belong, entirely and only to Him. . ." (8.20.49)

It was "heavenly" love: this was the adjective we used: this is what God wanted for us.

"Our love, that love, which must reign in our hearts, must be—because the Lord wants it this way—heavenly love, always a joyous love!. . . Let us not offend. . . this Love by complaining or with gloom, but at all times be prepared to overcome every pain with, and in, joy; that is God's will for us and we've got all the grace we need; the only thing is, to know how to make use of it. . ." (12.8.44)

This sort of life leads to a full experience of joy, to which we will now give some documentation:

"Among all the moments of the day prefer the painful ones (especially the inner feelings of being rejected and forsaken) because in these Jesus crucified and forsaken 'marries' the soul.

"This presence, always one made first and foremost by the will, very soon becomes *felt*, so that throwing ourselves into a sea of suffering we discover ourselves in a sea of love, of complete joy.

"We have confirmed through continuous experience that every pain of the soul (not of the body)* can be annulled, and the soul feels itself refilled with the Holy Spirit, who is joy, peace, serenity... I get more and more light on the possibility of overcoming the death of the soul this way (that is, any deprivation of love or of light, of joy or of peace), by means of this life which is CHRIST CRUCIFIED AND FORSAKEN..." (4.23.48).

"...(You have been) tested by pain and you know the flower of real joy which only grows from the ground of suffering. Today and just today I have learned that pain is the condition for the birth of that unique joy which can be born in a heart following Christ..." (6.29.45)

We knew the way to love Jesus Forsaken already in '45.

"Our soul is either in joy or in pain. When the soul is not singing, something is worrying it, and this something has to be given at once to God. The pains can come through external things..., they can also be interior pains (scruples, doubts, sadness, temptations, emptiness, nostalgia). All these pains have to be given to God. The swifter the gift, the sooner love descends into our hearts... If you feel something, whatever, which doesn't leave your soul alone in peace, whatever it is you must give it to Him... If you hold on to

---

* What is here described are experiences of the first stages of the spiritual life following the way of unity. They are also valid for later stages, except for particular moments or periods, as we shall say below.

something for yourself, even just the thought of the gift you've made, you are appropriating some riches to yourself (miserable riches!) which no longer belong to you" (4.15.45).

Pain was wiped out by doing that. Nevertheless we had to orient ourselves right away to living the will of God, well and fully, in the next moment.

Another letter reads:

". . . But get this straight, Father: to suffer pain of the soul is not at all essential to our vocation. There will be some. But we will have to overcome them, and we are always capable of doing it. Let Jesus Forsaken be everything to us, that is sufficient. . .

Rejoice in suffering with Him. Continue to love Him by doing His will. All pain passes away. Our vocation is unity, the fullness of joy." (5.10.48)

In '45 we added more specifically that the joy which fills the soul is kind of like the triumphal entry of God, a sort of Easter. Later on we will see how appropriate this definition is. ". . .only in extreme poverty of soul, a soul which loses itself for love, the Lord makes His triumphal entry with fullness of joy. That is why Easter meant to us a "Passover" into a life which is joy, which will know no sunset, as long as we live in conformity with the ideal we have chosen.

Would you like now to know our Eternal Model? Jesus crucified and forsaken. Filled up with the greatest pain known in heaven or on earth, the pain of God abandoned by God, His soul of the God-Man does not hesitate for a moment to offer it to His Father: "Father, into your hand I commend my spirit."[13]

69

We too must always do the same. And do you know what response Jesus will give to your offering? He'll give you everything, the whole fullness of His joy. . ." (4.15.45) And one comes to understand how the fruit of this love for Jesus Forsaken is being Jesus, living Jesus.

"I want to give you this further development of our thought, in order that the light of love may shine in you more brightly. Take everything that is yours at every moment and give it to Him. Give it to Him more and more immediately. The faster you give it to Him the sooner you will be Him. What greater thing could I tell you ? And what does life in love mean, if not to make a new copy of Him? If not to live him? Here is where our sanctity is: to arrive at being Him, so that we can say with St. Paul: 'It is no longer I who live, but Christ who lives in me' [14]"

Jesus Forsaken attracted us like a magnet, so that, right from the first months—this was still in 1944—, we felt ourselves drawn to put ourselves into the depths of his forsaken heart, which we identified as our proper place: right inside His wound, which we defined as 'new', because we thought of it as little known, not yet sufficiently "gutted". And once we were inside—we used to say—'beyond his wound', (that is having embraced Jesus Forsaken totally, so that we found ourselves beyond pain, in love) we felt like we were contemplating the immense love which God has poured out over the world. It is in fact from the pain of the Crucified, reaching its climax in that cry, that redemption comes, with sanctification and deification.

"Beyond the wound" we understood truly what love is, we were merged with love and shared in its light: the light of Love.

This was one way to express the vocation we felt to pass through abandonment in order to find God, who is Love.

"We who pursue this the most beautiful and attractive of ideals, have flung ourselves heart and soul into the new wound of His abandonment. In there we are secure, because we are living in the heart of our Love. Not only that, but from in there we see all the immensity of the Love of God poured out over the world. Put yourself as well (into the wound)...! You will find the light of Love, in other words it will become clear to you what Love is, because Jesus is the light of the world" (12.8.44)

To sum up: supernatural life, virtue, sweetness, fire, rest, consolation, fullness, companionship, peace, serenity, love, heavenly love, the light of Love, Love, Jesus, God: those are the extraordinary fruits of this life, of the love for Jesus Forsaken when, as we embrace Him, He—as we 've said—"weds our soul."

An already familiar page says:
"Jesus Forsaken embraced, hugged to oneself, chosen as our one and only all, consumed with us in one, while we are consumed in one with Him, and are turned into suffering with Him who is Suffering: this is everything. This is how you become (by participation) God, who is Love". ('49)

And today, after 40 years of the Focolare's life, these effects continue to exist, indeed they have even become an everyday matter.

We experience in our hearts, with the deepest gratitude to God, this continual flourishing of a Life ever new; in one's soul one is present at the repeated dawning of new light again and again, which clears everything away: doubts, distresses, worries—putting darkness to flight; we can be invaded with joys so heavenly that they shake our hearts to the depths, so that there's nothing left to do during the day but offer God holocausts of rejoicing: we notice the Holy Spirit is not far off, but within reach, our light and our guide.

People who are not involved in our Work * often recognize these realities in our members.

Important people of all the Christian churches, who have to travel around the world, sometimes say that they can distinguish members of the Focolare by the fruits of the Spirit which they believe they can see on their faces; they were struck, for example, not only by the witness to mutual love among the members, but especially by their joy.

III

So we have examined what it was we were discovering in Jesus Forsaken in the early days of the Focolare; we have seen where it was that He was found, and what our attitude had to be, and finally we have emphasized the various effects produced by love for Him.

Today we ask each other: what are these effects? How are these fruits to be classified?

When we spoke of unity, of our life of communion with our brethren, we understood that unity is Jesus, the Risen Christ. In unity Jesus' presence is felt, is seen, is enjoyed... All enjoy His presence, all suffer His absence. He is peace, joy, love, warmth, a climate of heroism, of extreme generosity. . ." And these effects and this atmosphere are the fruit of Jesus' Spirit, which is the Holy Spirit Himself. And the Spirit of Jesus Risen in our midst makes us become Jesus, and even to others we look like a continuation of Him, the Body of Christ, the Church.

In fact, anyone building unity through mutual love lives the death of Christ and His resurrection: that person "experiences" the life of the Risen One, which he or she possesses inside through grace. Consequently, they live the life which cannot die. Jesus says: ". . .whoever is alive and believes in me will never die."[15]

But we have noticed that also in embracing Jesus Forsaken, which any Christian can do, we experience effects equal to those of unity. In fact, identical effects.

What conclusion must be drawn? Granted that a Christian is not, and never can be, an isolated individual—can we infer that if we embrace Jesus Forsaken, the Risen Christ makes himself fully present

* The Work of Mary: Official name of the Focolare.

in each of us individually, with the same intensity, force, power, and total commitment with which He is in the midst of our complete unity?

Let's see what the Church has to say about it. And first of all, let's try to understand whether there may be some relationship between Jesus Crucified and Forsaken and the gift of the Holy Spirit.

The Gospel of St. John says: "When Jesus took the wine, he said, "Now it is finished." Then he bowed his head, and delivered over his spirit."[16]

The theologian Lyonnet makes the following comment on this passage: "St. John's expression, with reference to the death of Jesus, 'he bowed his head, and delivered over his spirit' (Jo, 19:30) is unusual. The verb 'delivered over' (his spirit) seems to have been chosen to indicate Christ's voluntary offering of His life... Using a very unusual expression to refer to Jesus' death, John meant to tell us that the effect of His death was the gift of the Spirit to the community".[17]

In the (Italian) ecumenical translation of the Bible we read: "John wished to suggest that it is by means of His death that Jesus is able to transmit the Spirit to the world".[18]

And Yves Congar writes: "...Jesus breathes upon Mary and John, who are as it were the Church at the feet of His cross. Jesus transmits the Spirit... Many Fathers interpreted it this way."[19]

Commenting on Jo. 7:39 St. Jerome says: "...The Spirit had not yet been given, because Jesus had not been glorified, that is He had not been crucified."[20]

St. Ambrose observes that "Christ crucified, thirsting, transfixed, the open rock from which flows water, fulfills what He promised in John 7:38: 'at that moment, therefore, He was thirsty, when from His side He poured forth rivers of living water sufficient to quench the thirst of all' "[21]. (Water symbolizes the Spirit.) St. Paul says Jesus became a curse in His (death on the) cross so that we might receive the promise of the Spirit.[22]

We read in the encyclical on The Mystical Body: ". . . through His blood the Church has been enriched with an abundant participation in His Spirit, . . ."

"With the shedding of His own blood on the cross Christ merited this Spirit for us . . ."[23] After Christ was glorified on the cross, His spirit was communicated to the Church, poured out abundantly"[24]. Clearly, therefore, a relationship exists between the crucified Jesus and the Spirit: Jesus procured Him for us on the cross. But, obviously, Jesus' cross coincides with His abandonment: if being forsaken is one of the pains of Jesus on the cross, indeed the climax of His pains, then we cannot speak of His pains, and of the cross, without thinking of His abondonment. To say, then, that there is a relation between the cross of Jesus and the Holy Spirit, is also to say that there is a relation between Jesus Crucified and Forsaken and the Holy Spirit.

All the same, though it is not yet affirmed by others, we can perhaps think that this particular pain of Jesus, His being forsaken, has a special relationship with the Holy Spirit. And this for the simple reason that when we give something away we have to feel its loss. On the cross Jesus felt, at that tremendous moment, His detachment from the Father. But who bonded Him and still bonds Him to the Father in a personal communion, if not the Holy Spirit Himself?

A theologian has said: "In the sacred texts the coming of the Holy Spirit is set in intimate relationship with the mystery of the passage of Christ to the Father. That mystery in fact fulfills the human love of the Incarnate Word in the most perfect way, a sign of the breath of love from which the Divine Spirit proceeds"[25].

But if the climax of the love of Jesus Crucified comes at His abandonment, that cry is where there is found "the most perfect realization of the human love of the incarnate Word." And so, we can also think that "the sign of the exhalation of love from which the Holy Spirit proceeds" is in Jesus' abandonment.

Anyhow—there is no reason to doubt the realationship between Jesus Crucified and Forsaken and the gift of the Holy Spirit.

So let's go a step further. Is the Holy Spirit given by Jesus through the cross given only to the community, or to individuals too?

Jesus has said: "If anyone thirsts, let him come to me; let him drink, who believes in me. Scripture has it: 'From within him rivers of living water shall flow.' "[26]

"Here he was referring to the Spirit, whom those that came to believe in him were to receive."[27] "From within him"—therefore from within the individual.

We read in St. Basil: ". . .The Holy Spirit is present in each person who receives Him, as though conferred on him alone. . ."[28]

Congar says: "The Holy Spirit is given to the community and is given to individuals. . ."[29]

These witnesses are enough to assure us that the Crucified gives the Holy Spirit to the individual Christian too.

We know what work the Holy Spirit does in each of us.

St. Paul says: "(God) brought us to life with Christ when we were dead in sin. By this favor you were saved. Both with and in Christ Jesus he raised us up and gave us a place in the heavens."[30]

Congar says: "During Jesus' human life, the Holy Spirit had in Him His temple, which included all mankind in expectancy and in the potential to assume them as children of God. Since the Lord's glorification, the Holy Spirit has this temple in us and in the Church. He accomplishes the same work in us of birth, (anothen: from above and anew, John 3:3), of life as members of the body of Christ, of the consummation of this quality in our very own body, in the glorious freedom of the sons of God (Rom. 8:21-23)."[31]

A theologian states: "In baptism the faithful are united to Christ who has died and is risen. In their intimate and real union, while still living in this world, they share in the heavenly triumph on the mystical level of grace and they await the manifestation of glory. Christians awakened to a new life and ideally in heaven, have changed their former being for a new one, that is, for the being of Christ. This radical change has come about by clothing themselves in Christ and sharing in his lot."[32]

Hence it is true that, through our embrace of Jesus Crucified and Forsaken, the Holy Spirit can pour out His gifts fully even in each one of us: it is true that the Risen One can manifest himself in each one of us.

We had already understood that, through the life of grace and our mutual love, we were living unity to the full, which is nothing other than the Risen One among us. Now we can affirm that, through the life of grace, which we each possess, and by embracing Jesus Crucified and Forsaken, in each of us individually the Risen One can live with his Spirit, in such a way that His effects can be experienced.

Thus we can say with the theologian, Cardinal Ratzinger: "The fount of the Spirit is Christ, the crucified. But, thanks to him, every Christian is a fount of the Spirit."[33]

We can get fresh proof of the presence of the Holy Spirit in the individual Christian, and therefore of His effects, from the saints.

In fact, looking more closely at "the will of God", we were able to note how these giants in the field of Religion who fulfilled this will by killing their own—embracing therefore the cross of renunciation and suffering—all experienced, they say "an ineffable beatitude... peace, tranquillity and a really heavenly bliss" (St. Frances Cabrini), "peace and calm" (St. Catherine of Siena), "a continual celebration" (St. Vincent De Paul). They experienced the fruits of the Spirit, among which is joy.

Joy! We mentioned joy in the first chapter, speaking about unity. Now we have seen how joy is an effect of our love for Jesus Forsaken, because it too is a fruit of the Spirit—joy which often manifests the other fruits, sums them up, crowns them; joy the flower of love, expression of life, of fullness, of consolation, of happiness, of beatitude; that joy which witnesses to light in the soul...

It has been said that joy is the uniform of the *focolarino*. And that is the way it is. It must be so. It cannot but be so, because the spirituality of the *focolarino* is unity and Jesus in his prayer for unity says: "that they may share my joy completely."[34]

Our joy, the joy of a Christian, in fact, is the joy of Jesus: not just the serene joy of children, certainly not the exuberance of the young which is purely human; not is it being cheerful, it is not an earthly happiness... Jesus has "his" joy, as he has "his" peace.

God wants "his" joy in the Christians, in the *focolarino*.

If we must be thoughtful and serious and sorrowful with those who are, normally we must be joyful, for joy is the open flower of love, it is the smile of love upon the world.

Every time that joy does not break into our hearts, we must ask ourselves: are we on the right road? Are we in the will of God?

But is joy *always* possible?

The testimonies that we have quoted are from the Focolare's early times, representing our first experiences.

Now many years have gone by, and certainly we are more mature. What do we think today?

First of all, we feel we must affirm that this fullness of joy, through embracing Jesus Forsaken, is the norm of our life: as we must experience in ourselves the death of Christ, sharing in his passion, so we must experience his resurrection in ourselves. And the Spirit—we saw—has led us by the hand and suggested as much as we needed to know for this to become a reality in our life.

This experience of death and resurrection, then, is made easier for us by our vocation to a community life, by our going to God together. We will never be able to estimate the help our brothers and sisters give us, even without knowing it. How much courage their faith infuses in us, how much warmth their love, how we are drawn ahead by their example! We will never know how to calculate the strength given to us by the presence of Christ in the community.

All the same, there can be particular moments, periods in life that are special, in which it is all but impossible to make joy penetrate our hearts, despite all our good will and the sincere embracing of Jesus Forsaken. They are dark moments, full of shadow, filled with the most varied spiritual pains, caused perhaps by psycho-somatic states, as we are often able to perceive. Or, more rarely, they are caused by true spiritual trials, genuine agonies, which the saints, for example, have experienced, and they are called "nights of the senses" and "nights of the spirit". These are Moments in which one is called to share the suffering of Jesus Forsaken in such a way as not to know how to say anything other than "Fiat" or "Thy will be done", with one's remaining strength. God permits them, as he permitted abandonment to his Son on the cross, but in us it is for our purification and our sanctification and, at times, to associate us with the redemptive work of Jesus.

If the painful moments exist, however, generally they do not regard the normal life of the *focolarino*. The *focolarini*, whatever their spiritual age, are called to live in joy, to have so much that they communicate to others. They are called to show to the world the Risen Christ inside themselves, besides His presence among them.

Using a metaphor typical of the times in which we were living, we used to say at a certain point in our story that Jesus Forsaken is like a machine: whoever is passed through it comes out Jesus. And we exhorted one another not to get stuck in the machine, in other words not to remain in suffering, but to allow the Risen One to let His life shine through us.

Now, this is just as true today: for the youngest who are just starting out on this road, for the one who has known it for a while, for those who are teachers of it, or ought to be.

It is sometimes noticeable, instead, that this joy is not there, or that it is not full. And this is certainly not because Jesus Forsaken is visiting the soul with particular trials, but because we have perhaps ceased to make him the favorite and exclusive love of our lives.

There is no resurrection without a death. There is no joy of Jesus without love for Jesus Forsaken.

There is no joy of Jesus without suffering which has been loved.

If we do not have the joy of the resurrection it means that Jesus Forsaken is no longer the ideal of our life, of our present moment. In his place there will be work, our ego (which wants to live when it must die), or study, activities, things, people . . .

In fact, the joy that God wishes to give us is special: it is the joy of the Risen Jesus, which blossoms from suffering, bursts out from renunciation, accompanies love.

And it is a contagious joy, one which can be distinguished from others, which impresses, attracts, converts. It is not a joy that you can just switch on, not a front you can use to fool yourself or others.

To possess it, then, it is necessary to choose and rechoose him every day and love him all the day long in the sufferings which come, in renunciations, in the mortifications required by our life as Christians and *focolarini,* in the penances which we cannot overlook.

Love Jesus Forsaken so that Jesus will live in us. Jesus Forsaken gave himself completely; in the spirituality which is centered on him, the Risen Jesus must shine out fully and our joy must witness to him.

In these chapters we have spoken of and quoted from several letters: of the documents left over from our early days, which speak of Jesus Forsaken, they are the most numerous.

But to whom were they written?

We wrote to our friends to draw them to the same ideal, to our parents and relatives, one by one: through them, also, we wanted to reach a lot more people. We wrote to priests, religious, and future religious. And as fire envelops all it touches, rejecting nothing and no one but grasping at everything with its flames, so does the spiritual fire burn in these letters.

"Look at him there where he is crucified and think: suppose it were your son? Hear him crying, 'My God, my God, why have you forsaken me?'.

It is the cry that echoes every moment in my heart. Think of him dying almost in despair and nailed up like a lamb—poor Jesus! Go on... tell me that you too love him and you want to make him loved by others! Tell me that, if I should die first, you will make your own the flame of my heart..." (25.12.44)

"In the name of him, crucified for Love of me and of you... accept the wishes I send you and make them yours: that love may make you understand how much he loved you and does love you! And stir up in your heart my passion of Love..." (25.12.44)

"You too... hurry to love Jesus Crucified and Forsaken by everybody, even by his Father... Have my ideal which is him: Jesus Forsaken, and do all you can to see to it that He will be forsaken no more, either by you or by any of those who pass your way in life.

Look around you and see how many souls there are. Try to help them love this Love, which must save the world. Make friends with your sister's friends and tell them to love this Forsaken Love and everything else will be 'added unto them'. But 'everything else' doesn't matter. What matters is only to love Love!..." (undated)

God urges us, therefore, to open everyone's eyes. As all were candidates for unity, all had to know the one who had paid for it , who is its key.

Nobody should remain indifferent, but all had to be aware of how much Jesus loved us.

His cry was for everyone!

From the very beginning, in fact, our hearts felt a mission!

"...you know that my Love has called me to carry out a great mission.

I must, I desire to make him loved by all the world, because it was for my sake that he was crucified and forsaken!

And you... have pity on this Jesus who continues to knock at your heart to get some consolation from you!

You must, you can embrace my ideal! Even if your way is a little different from mine..." (1.1.45)

We felt urged then, to speak of him to everybody.

We felt the vocation to create around him, as we called it, "a paradise of stars".

To a girl, to whom we had given the name Eli *, we wrote as early as 1945:

"...Cry out (which meant: live!) your name to the Eternal Father and to the heart of the Virgin! Cry it out for the whole of humanity, for every sinner of the world,

* Derived from: "Eli, Eli lema sabacthani"(Mt 27,46) (Hebrew: My God, my God, why have you forsaken me?)

for our girls... Cry it out from the depths of your heart. 'But, why, my God, have you forsaken me?'

Cry it out as if you were Jesus, because the heavenly Father and the mother of Jesus and of us, cannot hear that cry without coming to our aid! We have such great need of help from heaven to form on earth 'a paradise of stars' for Jesus Forsaken!'' (10.30.45)

Those were certainly moments of a particular grace; the letters are there to give witness to it. But they were moments which, perhaps in other ways, we are called to relive even today, and we can do it fully if it is not we who live, but the Risen One who lives in us. Through him (we understood) we too have become sources of the Spirit. We too are other Jesuses. And, if this is true, his word: "I came to cast fire upon the earth..."[35] becomes ours as well. We too can and must be fire for this world.

Let us, therefore, announce Jesus Forsaken to all, do our best to extend and make flourish the vineyard of Jesus Forsaken, namely the Focolare, which is the realization, today, of the "paradise of stars" mentioned above.

Announce Jesus Forsaken, however, at the right moment.

While the two faces of the coin of our Ideal have been, from the beginning, Jesus Forsaken and unity, this is the way the Spirit urged us to go forward: immediately offer other people our unity, but preserve Jesus Forsaken to ourselves.

"I show the page of unity to everyone. For myself and for those who are in the front line of unity, our one ALL

IS JESUS FORSAKEN...

To the others unity, for us the abandonment. What abandonment? That which Jesus... has suffered... 'My God, my God, why have you forsaken me?"

To seek him like the bride in the Song of Songs is our highest duty, we who have been cast by the infinite love into the front line..." (30.3.48)

The first witness to give to the world is that of unity. Whoever is touched by it will know how to grasp its secret.

Indeed, for anyone who chooses unity the encounter with Jesus Forsaken happens of necessity.

"Ah, brother! If you plunge yourself into this way (of unity), you will soon experience the stigmata of the abandonment! Then the Lord will dig out of your heart an infinite void... which you will fill immediately with Jesus Forsaken..." (30.3.48)

With these wisdom-filled suggestions the Holy Spirit really got us started on the mission, which our Movement has in the Church and the world: to contribute to "that all may be one" by means of a dialogue of love with everybody, a dialogue which is possible and constructive if it is preceded by witness. Dialogue, therefore, about Someone who has already been experienced, at least a little: God, who manifests himself in unity, so that we learn to discover the love in the incarnation, in the cross, in the abandonment, so that all of us may clothe ourselves in this love, and become identified with it so that, more and more, we may radiate in this world the Risen Jesus.

JESUS FORSAKEN;
KEY TO UNITY
WITH OUR NEIGHBORS

Jesus Forsaken is not only a way for and a key to our soul's unity with God. He is also the key to unity with our neighbors, to the way to love them, to the manner for brothers and sisters to love one another.

And this is an essential topic for us of the Focolare.

It is well known that the choice of God-Love, from the moment this new life came to be, meant to choose the way of love. In a truly divine synthesis, the Spirit made us recognize immediately all that Jesus desired from us in this characteristic commandment of his: "I give you a new commandment: Love one another".[36]

Unity with other people, unity between people, is therefore a subject of extreme importance for us. It is not by chance that when we are asked what we are, we are often at a loss to find any better way of replying than telling the little story of our beginnings: the collapse of everything during the war, the choice of God and, to live up to that choice, the practice of this commandment.

We are always returning to this demand of Jesus as to the first and fundamental inspiration, it fascinates us, attracts us we rediscover it as new everytime we consider it more closely; living it we feel that we are in our element.

We are filled with enthusiasm when we realise that if it is a subject of such great importance to us, little children of the Church, the same was true for the Church when it began ("This, remember, is the message you heard from the beginning, we should love one another," says John)[37] as it is of great importance also for the Church of today.

Vatican II specifies that the law of the new people of God is the commandment of love. In love, indeed, there is not just one law of Christ, but the whole of *his* law. Scripture has always affirmed that: "he who loves his neighbor has fulfilled the law."[38] "The whole law has found its fulfillment in this one saying: "You shall love your neighbor as yourself." "[39]

Love, charity, participation in that *agape* which is God's own life ("God is agape"),[40] is the highest mark of Christianity; in fact, it is the whole of our religion.

The Christian who is freed from all slavery by the Spirit living in him or her, bringing the fruits of "love, joy, peace, patient endurance, kindness, generosity, faithfulness, gentleness",[41] becomes, precisely because of this same Spirit, the slave of someone: of his or her neighbor. the Christian lives life paying a perennial debt: that of serving other people.[42]

And this love that Christ commands we have for other people, the service he commands, is not made up merely of acts, one after another, but it is like a state of being in which Christians come to find ourselves, a state in which we reach our perfection in the best way possible. Service of one's neighbor, in fact, is the way, par excellence, of Christian perfection. "Love binds the rest together and makes them perfect."[43]

Although Vatican II gives the example of the vows of Religious Life as an effective way of reaching sanctity, it does not hesitate to set service of one's neighbor above them,[44] because love for one's neighbor is in truth the specific characteristic of the Christian: St. Paul, moreover, puts love above all charisms.[45]

And so, if the Church thinks this way, and if this is exactly what the Holy Spirit taught directly to our hearts, we can understand how important it is to know the best way to love our brothers and sisters, the most appropriate way to achieve unity with them.

Jesus said: "This is my commandment, love one another" but he did not leave this love without a model, for he added, "as I have loved you."[46] And he did not leave this without any explanation when he added further: "There is no greater love than this, to lay down one's life for one's friends."[47]

Yes, Jesus Crucified and Forsaken is the way to love our neighbor. His death on the cross, forsaken, is the highest, divine, heroic lesson from Jesus as to the nature of love.

This vision of Jesus Crucified and Forsaken is what the Holy Spirit has branded on the hearts of the members of the Focolare so that they may know the meaning of love. They conform their lives to him, as much as their weakness allows.

We have already seen above, how loving means to serve and how there is no better way of serving than 'to make ourselves one' with our neighbors.

No one has equalled Jesus Forsaken, in making himself one with his neighbors. For this reason, he is the model of the person who loves, He is the path and the key to unity with our neighbors.

"To make ourselves one".

But what is meant and what is required by these few short words, which are so important as to stand for the way to love?

We cannot enter the heart of another person to comprehend them, to understand them, to share their suffering, if our spirit is rich with a worry, a judgment, a thought... with anything at all. "Making ourselves one" demands spirits that are poor, poor in spirit. Only with people like this is unity possible.

And who, then, do we look to in order to learn this great art of being poor in spirit, this art which (as the gospel tells) brings with it the Reign of God, the kingdom of love, love in the soul? We look to Jesus Forsaken. No one is poorer than he: he, having lost nearly all of his disciples, having given his mother away, gives also his life for us and experiences the terrible sensation that his Father has abandoned him.

Looking at him we understand how everything is to be given or put aside for love of our neighbors: the things of this earth must be given away or put aside and also—should it be necessary—in a certain way, the things of heaven. In fact, looking at him who felt himself forsaken by God, when love for other people asks it (and this can happen often) we must be ready even to leave God for God, as we say—God, for example, in prayer, to "make ourselves one" with someone in need; giving up God in that which seems to us to be our inspiration, in order to be completely empty and receive into ourselves another's suffering. Looking at him, every renunciation is possible.

And "making ourselves one" implies this renunciation, even if we know what the gain will be. Other people who are loved thus are often won over to Christ ("To the weak I became a weak person, with a view to winning the weak. I have made myself all things to all men, in order to save at least some of them.")[48] And, once they are won over, they too love and then, there is unity.

The Focolare Rule says: "The life of union among the faithful . . . demands of its members a very special love for the cross and in particular for Jesus in the mystery of his passion: the divine model for all those who want to work together for the union of all with God and with one another, *the highest point of external deprivation but above all of inward. . .*"[49] and it goes on to cite the cry of Jesus: "My God, my God, why have you forsaken me?".

It is Jesus Forsaken, therefore, who is the cause of unity.

Jesus Forsaken, however, is the way to unity with our neighbors in another way.

Jesus says: "I living in them, you living in me, that their unity may be complete."[50]

Thus it is Jesus present in every Christian, who makes them perfectly one.

But how is it possible for Jesus to fulfill in us His "I living in them"?

We have looked closely at this when speaking about Jesus Forsaken, as key to the soul's unity with God. It is necessary to embrace him always, generously and without hesitation when he presents himself in the sufferings of each day, in the renunciations which the Christian life and all the virtues involve.

Then the Risen One, who we hope is already in us by grace, shines out in all his splendor; the gifts of the Spirit flow into our souls: it is an Easter that is celebrated again and again; Jesus lives in each one of us fully.

But if Jesus lives in me, and he lives also in my neighbor, it is obvious that, when I meet my neighbor, we are already one, we are perfectly one.

And what has made this possible? Love for Jesus Forsaken.

Jesus Forsaken is also the way of unity with our neighbor because he helps us to rebuild unity each time it has been shattered. In fact, it can happen that we have already experienced that full joy, that peace, that light, that ardor, that readiness to love, all those fruits of the Spirit which are produced by the New Commandment when it is put into practice. It may be, that is, that we already know what is implied by the presence of Jesus among two or more Christians who are united in his name. And we have experienced what tremendous meaning it gives to our existence, even in its details: how it has shed light on circumstances, things and people. But all of a sudden, an act of pride, arrogance or a speck of selfishness on the part of one or the other, makes us plunge back into an existence similar to that which we had before knowing Jesus more fully, an existence without warmth and color, or even worse than that. An uneasiness invades our soul; everything loses meaning: we do not understand why we began to live this way. The most important element is missing: he who made our life full, who had made us brim full of joy, is missing. It is as if a supernatural sun had gone down.

What can we do?

In that moment only the memory of the black forsakenness into which his divine soul had been plunged, can give us light. Would not all Jesus'life, which had been lived entirely for his Father, lose its value for him if, at the climax of his offering, his Father abandoned him? What sense was there in dying now? But he did not doubt: "Father, into your hands I commend my spirit!"[51]

Troubled as our souls are by a small or large disunity, aware of sharing a little in that agony of his, we go deep into our hearts and we embrace our suffering and then: we run to our brother or sister to rebuild full harmony—whether we or they were the guilty party (the Gospel, when it asks us not to bring our gift to the altar before being reconciled with our brother, does not distinguish between the guilty and the innocent). And Jesus returns among us, bringing with him strength and happiness again.

Jesus Forsaken is always the key to every unity that is re-established.

Jesus in his abandonment is the path to unity with our neighbor also in another way—a mysterious one, but real.

He said: "I, once I am lifted up from the earth, will draw all men to myself";[52] that is, I will make all one.

If it is true that Christ lives in the Christian, the Christian can, in a certain way, repeat this word about himself or herself. We don't know how much has been contributed to unity by those living crucifixes who, day by day, are raised by God's will upon the cross of brief or lasting illnesses or even deaths offered for the Focolare. God knows. Certainly their gift is always of tremendous worth if, in the divine economy, suffering is the most fruitful element.

But who do all these people look to as they offer their Mass for the aims of the Focolare? They look to him, to whose Passion they unite their own, so that all mankind "may be one".

Jesus Forsaken, lastly, is the cause of unity with our neighbor also because we see him, some semblance of him, in all those who suffer. We see him in those who are troubled, in society's rejects, in the persecuted, in the needy, in those who suffer hunger and thirst, in the naked, sick, dying, in the homeless. We see him in prisoners: who is more a prisoner and pinned down than he, in a bodily sense but also in his soul, because of the terrifying sensation that he has been abandoned by the Father with whom he is perfectly one?

We see him in those who doubt. What greater doubt than his, when, for us, he seems to believe the absurdest of absurdities: that God forsakes God?

94

We see him in the afflicted, in the disconsolate, in the forsaken, in failures, in the betrayed, in outcasts, in the victims of unsuccess or of impossible situations, in the disorientated, in the defenceless or desperate or those drowned in fear...

We see him also in the sinner, because for us he made himself sin, a curse.[53]

In all of these persons, in all those who suffer pain of soul or body, it is not difficult to recognize his face. And because we see his face, we love him.

Thus, his figure, that these suffering people recall, is the cause of our love. Jesus Forsaken is the pathway to unity with them. And then, once loved, more often than not, they love in their turn. And unity is achieved.

Hence it is very understandable that the members of the Focolare, because they love Jesus Forsaken, are open to love the whole of humanity and to direct people—in the places where they meet them—towards the "ut omnes;" "that all may be one".

Indeed, they feel so deeply the need of this love for him that it has in the course of time become a practice for all of them, for decades now, to "consecrate themselves" to Jesus Forsaken. Those who have greater responsibility do so, like the *focolarini*, the priests, the religious, the married people, the volunteers. The young people do so as well. Even the children do so.

They all understand that here is the key of their Ideal.

Therefore they vow themselves to Jesus Forsaken, as a way of making an explicit vow to love, because he is love.

But the Focolare loves Jesus Forsaken in humanity not only through its individual members, but also as a whole and in its parts. The various mass movements,* for example, love Jesus Forsaken in the respective problems they deal with, problems which always manifest one of his faces.

Because of him, the New Families Movement, for instance, finds itself successfully coping with the problems of orphans: who is more the figure of an orphan than Jesus in that moment on the cross? Or coping with widows: who is more alone than He, without protection or company? And likewise also for the problems of separations, of divorces, of old people, of the generation gap etc.

Because of him, the New Humanity Movement strives to solve the thousands and thousands of problems for humanity in the various sectors of social life: in the world of work—the problems of unemployment, of the tensions between social classes etc; in the political world—the problems of human rights, of the relationship between parties and so on.

Because of him, it works to give a reply to the world's problems in health and education: who is more similar to those in need of instruction, than Jesus, the Word of God, who for us made himself ignorance in his "why"?

* The "mass movements" are those listed in the following paragraphs. (cf. Chiara Lubich, *Scritti Spirituali* III, pp 110-111)

Because of him, the Priests' Movement offers a solution to the problems of priests, of those who are too lonely, or old, of the sometimes insufficient communion among them, of their duty to be united to the bishops; to the problems of vocations, of seminaries... The Parishes Movement seeks to respond to all of the problems the Church presents in a parish, with its liturgical ceremonies, with its multiplicity of activities and its associations, but especially with the need it bears within itself to be a living communion.

Because of him, the Movements of men and women Religious know how to offer an answer to the many problems of religious families: the renewal of their spirit, the return to the observance of their Rule, the unity between religious and their superiors, vocations, the unity between the various religious families.

Because of him, the young people's movements (the Gen, the New Youth Movement...) give a hand to the solution of the grave problems of young people and children today.

The Focolare, however—and it is necessary to underline this—does not have as its direct aim the renewal of the family, of youth, or of the various spheres of society. Nor does it have as its immediate goal that of solving the problems of religious families, of priests, of seminarians, of parishes... even though in practice, it contributes towards solving and renewing all of these.

The aim of the Focolare is to contribute towards the realization of Jesus' last will and testament in the world. To accomplish this end it has mass movements (which aim at the youth, families, parishes, society, priests, religious): to create, to form a single tissue of the various components of the Christian world and to show to the world what the Church is when Christ, the Risen One, is in the midst of his children.

This is the way that the Focolare feels it can share the present concerns and sufferings of the Church, above all by giving a witness of unity, with the presence of Christ, and with his Spirit which renews everything (a witness which is the basis of every other activity in the field of the apostolate).

For us the various regions of the Third World to which the Church gives so much care and attention (where there are so many needs or possibilities, but the laborers are few) these regions, too are an echo of the cry of Jesus Forsaken to which we attempt to respond in some way.

Likewise, the Church of Silence is to our hearts like one great Jesus crying out his forsaknenness. With this in mind, the words of a bishop from one of those countries, when he heard us speaking of this aspect of Jesus' Passion, are always present to us: "Jesus Forsaken is how the Church lives its Passion today."

And so we come to the three possibly most important objectives of the Church today, for which, after the Second Vatican Council, it has opened three great dialogues.

In the course of its forty years' history, the Focolare has also come to recognize its principal aims in the same objectives: the reunion of Christians; the dialogue with other religions; the encouter with the wide-spread problem of atheism in the world.

The Focolare's spirituality (as we have been discovering through experience) contains extremely useful elements for dialogue with the various Churches. And these have enabled us to open and to develop a constructive dialogue with Christians of various denominations, so that something truly ecumenical has been born.

These elements are: *love* as the core component of Christianity and *life* ("Your way is a way of life," said Pope John Paul II) which have touched our Orthodox brothers and sisters; *the word of God* which we stress in a very special way, and which has begun a dialogue and a communion, that is indeed, profound, with the Lutherans; *unity,* which particularly interests our Anglican brothers and sisters, starting, from their authorities; Jesus' words, *"Where two or more are gathered in my name, there am I in their midst",* which has been the key word in our dialogue with members of the Reformed Churches, and so on.

Because of these various elements, which we share in common with Christians of other Churches or ecclesial communities, the Focolare has been able to gather abundant fruit, such as, the collapse of centuries-old prejudices on either side, the acceptance of truths professed by the Catholic church by other Christians, for our part a more objective evaluation of many situations and in everyone an overpowering desire for unity.

But it has been above all for the sake of Jesus Forsaken that we have been able to construct something in this field.

His figure disfigured (Jesus Forsaken in terrible anguish because of the uncertainty, so to speak, of his unity with the Father, appears really to be like the anti-figure of Him who was always so sure of that unity), his figure disfigured has been the thing we have always seen in the Christian world, called originally to the most perfect unity, it is now subdivided into hundreds of Churches.

It is for him, for his cry which is raised up by so many traumas, divisions, separations, that the Focolare feels mobilized to work for the restoration of unity in the Church.

The spread of the Focolare all over the world, then, has brought it into frequent contact with the faithful of other religions: with Jews, with Muslims, with Buddhists, with Jaoists, with Sikhs, with Hindus etc. And with all of them we have found something to link us.

While we are united to the Jews by the priceless inheritance of the Old Testament, while Muslims find interesting our living the faith as a community, not just as individuals (given their idea of religious life), to the faithful of Eastern Religions we are bound in a very special way by Jesus Forsaken. The others, too, are curious: we have often heard Jews affirm, having come to know this culmination of Jesus' Passion, "Then, this man was truly God."[54]

But to the faithful of theEasternReligions that typical suffering of Jesus, which brought him to out-and-out annihilation, gives rise to a very special fascination.

Often, in fact, by means of the mortification of their senses and of every desire, they seek that "energy" (as they call it) which is the ground of everything, or God, whom sometimes they love as a person. And their asceticism is admirable. It carries them so high, that they are able to have a certain perception of Christian supernatural life, when they meet genuine Christians. It is "being", in fact, which has value for them. And when someone dies to self in order to "make him or herself one" with them and consequently lets Christ live in him or herself, or when they came into contact with the Risen One in the midst of Christians who are united, they know how to distinguish that light and that peace, effects of the Spirit, which shine from their faces: they are attracted and they ask for an explanation. This leads to speaking of our religion: dialogue which becomes evangelization.

And there is a third dialogue, one which is also very special, to which the Focolare feels itself called. It is the dialogue with non-believers, with those who are far off, with atheists, with materialists.

We consider, in fact, that it would have been meaningless for the Focolare to be called to make Jesus' greatest suffering its own, if it were not to dedicate itself, in the midst of humanity, to the most wretched of all people.

And the most wretched, the most destitute are not even those who are dying of hunger; rather they are those who, after this life, will not know the other, because they have rejected God or because they have put material things in his place.

To dedicate ourselves to them, whom we find not only in countries which are well-known for being atheist, but who can be met in the West as in the East, in big cities as in little villages, is, it seems to us, the first and foremost call of the Focolare; a call which is so characteristically ours, so special, that it makes us think that the other dialogues, like that with non-Catholic Christians, are made to serve this one.

And so; to love. To love all mankind, so that all may know the nature of love and may love one another as Jesus desired—this is the yearning of the Focolare.

Hence in the times in which it has been born, times caressed by the powerful breath of the Holy Spirit, but also threatened by atomic warfare, the Focolare has its secret: Jesus Forsaken, he who rejoined human beings to God and to one another. With its sprirituality centered around him, a true "divine atomic bomb", as our Gen call it (it seems in that cry indeed that unity, itself, which is God, is shattered; for it is God who cries out: "My God, my God why have you forsaken me?"!), with this spirituality the Focolare feels itself to be living in unison with the Church of our times and to be able to pursue with the Church its goal of today and forever: to fulfill Jesus' last will and testament: "That they may all be one."[55]

NOTES

[1] Psalm 2:8
[2] 1 Co 9:19
[3] Cf. Jn 17:10, 21,22
[4] Mt 28:20
[5] Cf. Jn 14:21
[6] From an ancient hymn
[7] Mt 18:20
[8] 1 Pt 4:8
[9] Jn 17:29
[10] Jn 17:13
[11] Cf. Lk 12:32
[12] Mt 27:46
[13] Lk 23:46
[14] Gal 2:20
[15] Jn 11:26
[16] Jn 19:30
[17] S. Lyonnet, *Il Nuovo Testamento alla luce dell'
Antico*, Brescia 1970, p. 92, cit. in *Il Vangelo di
Giovanni*, a commento by B. Maggioni, in *I Vangelo*,
Assissi 1975 p. 1671-1672.
[18] Traduzione Ecumenica della Bibbia: Nuovo
Testamento; loc. cit.

[19] Yves Congar *Je crois en l'Espirit Saint*, I, Paris 1979, p. 79.

[20] Quoted in H. Rahner, *L' ecclesiologia dei Padri*, Rome, 1971, p. 380

[21] Ibid p. 388

[22] Cf. Gal 3:13ff

[23] Pius XII, *Mystici Corporis*

[24] Ibid

[25] M. Bordoni, *Il tempo: valore filosofico e mistero teologico*, Rome 1965, p. 141-142

[26] Jn 7:37-38

[27] Jn 7:39

[28] St. Basil *Liber de Spiritu Sancto* IX, 22

[29] Yves Congar *Credo nello Santo*, II, Brescia 1982 p.22 and 25

[30] Eph 2:5-6

[31] Yves Congar *op. cit.* p. 77-78

[32] Elio Peretto, *Commento alla lettera agli "Efesini"*, in *Il Nuovo Testamento*, II, Ed. Paoline, 1977, p. 654

[33] J. Ratzinger, *Lo Spirito Santo come "communio"*, in *La riscoperta dello Spirito Santo*, Milan 1977, p. 258

[34] Cf. Jn 17:13

[35] Lk 12:49

[36] Jn 13:34

[37] 1 Jn 3:11

[38] Ro 13:8

[39] Gal 5:14

[40] 1 Jn 4:8

[41] Gal 5:22-23

[42] Cf. Ro 13:8

[43] Col 3:14

[44] Cf. L.G. 42
[45] Cf. 1 Cor 13
[46] Jn 15:12
[47] Jn 15:13
[48] 1 Cor 9:22
[49] Part I, Ch. 1, art. 2-10
[50] Jn 17:23
[51] Lk 23:46
[52] Jn 12:32
[53] Cf. Gal 3:13
[54] Cf. Mk 15:39
[55] Jn 17:21